Praise for *Sticky Teaching :*

Caroline's non-patronising explanations outline key ideas with clarity, bringing the concept of sticky teaching and learning to life. She also offers thoughtful reflection points throughout, encouraging teachers to ask questions of their own practice. Her helpful toolkit also offers practical, evidence-based strategies to help challenge and support students.

Humphrey Waddington, Assistant Head Teacher, North London Collegiate School

In this book, Caroline has captured the essence of making teaching memorable with plenty of great ideas for the new teacher as well as those looking for new approaches to top up their toolkit. A well thought-out, research-informed and realistic addition to the professional library.

Hywel Roberts, writer, teacher, speaker and humorist

Packed full with relevant, relatable and realistic classroom ideas, Caroline's book is accessible, engaging and perfect for the busy classroom teacher. I love the concept of sticky teaching, as it offers a refreshing take on teaching and pedagogy. I will, without a doubt, be using these strategies in my own lessons.

Kate Lewis, Assistant Head Teacher, Arthur Mellows Village College

Sticky Teaching and Learning is for all those teachers who have taught a great lesson on Monday, yet, by Tuesday, their pupils' knowledge appears to have simply evaporated overnight. Throughout the book, Caroline Bentley-Davies provides startling insights and thoughtful perspectives on evidence-based techniques for improving retention and recall and securing learning by locking knowledge into the long-term memory bank so that pupils' learning lingers. Furthermore, Caroline's voice is wonderfully energetic, engaging and mercifully free of educational gabble. Needless to say, this book really stuck with me!

**Sarah Martin, School Improvement Adviser and
Director of Teacher Education, The Active Learning Trust**

After attending Caroline's course on sticky teaching, I was delighted at the prospect of having a handbook containing her words of wisdom and guidance. Caroline truly understands the struggles that both pupils and teachers have with consolidating knowledge and effectively improving learning. The practical ideas that feature in this book have been useful and beneficial for all the pupils I teach. They allow you to have fun with teaching, but you are also reassured that they aren't there just to tick boxes during a formal observation so that the lesson looks 'good' – they actually do benefit the pupils. Caroline's focus on metacognition lends itself well to a range of easy-to-use techniques, which will help pupils with their learning throughout their education and beyond. Her strategies have really changed the dynamic in my classroom. The love for learning has returned!

Naomi Boyd, Head of Upper Sixth, Emanuel School

Sticky Teaching and Learning is essential reading for all teachers who want to make their lessons and learning as sticky as possible. Perfect for the time-pressed teacher who wants useful and practical techniques to make the learning stick, the book shares a wealth of successful pupil-tested classroom strategies that are underpinned by both research and background philosophy. Each sticky strategy also comes with a clear and concise explanation of what to do and why it works. Caroline shows you how to make what you teach really stick, and guides you through planning, questioning, review and assessment – to help your students to become more resilient and effective learners.

Lesley Ann McDermott, Head of History, Whitworth Park Academy

Sticky Teaching and Learning is incredibly inspiring. It uses examples from teachers to offer some really powerful ways of increasing pupils' motivation, boosting their self-esteem and encouraging them to be aspirational in their learning. A whole-school CPD package in one book.

Brenda Parker, Assistant Principal, The Pingle Academy, and Lead for ECT and ITT teacher training, The de Ferrers Trust

Sticky Teaching and Learning offers an excellent blend of theory and practice. Its research-informed content is supported by case studies and examples which illustrate how to embed the strategies that Caroline shares into your practice immediately. The book offers a smorgasbord of quick wins for newly qualified and experienced teachers alike, and the ready-to-use toolkit of 50 techniques makes this easy to implement too. Caroline's conversational tone also encourages professional reflection and development, as reading it feels a bit like chatting with a teaching guru over a coffee.

Jeni Loud, Assistant Deputy Head (Staff), Lord Wandsworth College

In *Sticky Teaching and Learning*, Caroline Bentley-Davies shares her experience of teaching and promotes the autonomy, independence and rights of children to be learners. She shares with teachers a range of approaches for keeping learning alive and for encouraging pupils to be brave in their learning while nurturing a healthy self-reliance. Caroline encourages both children and staff to not fear imperfections or incorrect answers, but rather to see them as part of the perfection of the art of learning. Such a mindset brings benefits to staff who model behaviours as lifelong learners, thus creating a class climate where all can flourish. The book also offers a wealth of evidence-based research and a comprehensive bibliography which will support further study.

Christian N. Kendall-Daw, Deputy Head Teacher, St George's Weybridge

In a time of real concern over 'lost learning' due to the enforced lockdowns and school closures of the COVID-19 pandemic, *Sticky Teaching and Learning* is the toolkit we have all been waiting for. It draws on a range of engaging examples, current educational research and theories and a range of effective practices to really make the reader think about how to engage pupils as active participants in their learning.

Making the precious curriculum content we have delivered stick is the thing we all crave – and this book presents practical and accessible strategies in a really readable format to enable us, as teachers, to do just that.

Charlotte Cross, Assistant Head Teacher – Teaching and Learning,
Bournville School

Given that a need to make learning memorable is integral to effective teaching, Caroline Bentley-Davies' *Sticky Teaching and Learning* is important reading for new and experienced teachers alike. It is, in fact, a comprehensive manual, offering structured guidance on all aspects of classroom practice – from creating a purposeful environment, to effective planning, questioning, feedback, mindset, and more. Her tone will be familiar to anyone who has had the opportunity to work with her in her capacity as an adviser, combining as it does the authority which comes from meticulous research and plenty of experience in the classroom, as well as a very real appreciation of the challenges faced by both students and teachers.

Anthony Lowey, English teacher and Progress Leader,
Stratford upon Avon School

Caroline Bentley-Davies

Sticky
Teaching
and Learning

How to make your students remember what you teach them

Crown House Publishing Limited
www.crownhouse.co.uk

First published by

Crown House Publishing Ltd
Crown Buildings, Bancyfelin, Carmarthen, Wales, SA33 5ND, UK
www.crownhouse.co.uk

and

Crown House Publishing Company LLC
PO Box 2223, Williston, VT 05495, USA
www.crownhousepublishing.com

British Library of Cataloguing-in-Publication Data
A catalogue entry for this book is available from the British Library.

Print ISBN 978-178583535-3
Mobi ISBN 978-178583571-1
ePub ISBN 978-178583572-8
ePDF ISBN 978-178583573-5

LCCN 2021937455

Printed and bound in the UK by
Charlesworth Press, Wakefield, West Yorkshire

For my parents – thank you so much for encouraging me.

Acknowledgements

I would like to thank the entire Crown House team for their hard work and for all their expertise, in particular: David Bowman, Beverley Randell, Amy Heighton and Emma Tuck.

Thank you to Ross, my amazing husband, for his consistent support and wonderful ideas.

Thanks to the thousands of fantastic teachers I have met who have shared tips and teaching ideas with me. Special thanks to: Jo Baker, Charlotte Cross, Vanessa Lea, Kate Lewis, Lesley Ann McDermott and Dr Paul Owen, and for general writing and lockdown support: Kelly Hudson and Jo Noble.

Preface

This book has come about for several reasons. I teach pupils and teachers in the UK and overseas, and I know it is important not just that I 'feel' my teaching has gone well but that it really influences my pupils. It matters that they remember and can draw on the learning in later lessons and in later life. I write training courses on all aspects of teaching and learning; however, recently teachers have been clamouring for training on how to help their pupils remember their lessons – essentially, how to make learning stick.

The need to make our teaching 'sticky' has never been greater. Coursework, once the fail-safe of the conscientious pupil, has gone. No longer can coursework or long-term assessments be carefully polished or redone if they are not deemed successful enough. Pupils are therefore increasingly reliant on their own ability to remember and utilise knowledge. Sometimes they will have been taught the course material over two years previously, but they still need to retain this information 24 months later at some speed and under immense pressure. We need to make knowledge sticky. Our pupils must be skilled at retrieving, shaping and utilising what we have taught them, so that in an assessment they can prove exactly what they know and can do. We can't afford to sell them short.

There are other reasons why we want pupils to become successful at sticky learning. We want them to develop an appetite and aptitude for learning that will stay with them for the rest of their lives. We want them to enjoy learning and relish the challenge of mastering new skills and knowledge. We want to give them lifelong skills in developing successful learning strategies for themselves. As educators, there is an increasing rebellion against *just* preparing pupils for the demands of a specific test or examination. In some schools, in recent years pupils have been force-fed information, a foie gras approach to education if you like, a fail-safe for examination success.

These passive pupils are stuffed full of facts, information and enough pass notes to enable them to hurdle over the examination requirements with the minimum of effort. Countless revision sessions and notes are provided for pupils by their teachers. There is little expectation that they will develop any autonomy or the will to revise and learn for themselves or by themselves.

This wasn't the intention, of course. However, in increasingly accountable times teachers and school leaders have been under immense pressure to get results – at any cost. Of course, we want pupils to pass tests and become successful. However, the over-reliance of pupils on their teachers means that they become much less skilled at learning and thinking independently. Instead, they are increasingly reliant on their teachers' efforts, rather than their own. Ultimately, it doesn't work. It doesn't get the best results and it doesn't help to secure learning.

A classic example of the danger inherent in this practice occurred when I was observing some students in a school near Essex. The school was working incredibly hard to get them to achieve well in their examinations. I observed a hard-working teacher with one reluctant GCSE class. Her lesson was well prepared and she had excellent subject knowledge, but the students were sluggish and apathetic throughout the lesson. This was a crucial lesson: it covered essential learning points and reviewed some of the key material they would need for their examinations, which were just a few weeks away. However, when I challenged one lad about why he was not paying full attention and engaging with the activities, his reply was very telling: 'It's alright, Miss. We've got revision classes after school today and Miss will go through it all again.' The students knew that the lesson would be rerun like a Netflix episode, allowing for minimal mindless participation in the first instance. The students could allow it to wash over them because it would be repeated immediately after school! They didn't need to make any real effort with their learning.

One of the key premises of sticky teaching is that the initial learning in the lesson must actively involve pupils. They can't simply be passive observers.

Instead they must be active participants in the actual learning in the lesson. There are of course several advantages to this. Firstly, if pupils are active participants in their own learning, they are more likely to engage, remember and reflect on what they have learned. Moreover, when teaching pupils who are just unreceptive recipients of the teachers' knowledge, it is hard – if not impossible – to tell how much has been properly understood and retained. You can't tell what learning is insecure and will require revisiting and reteaching because the pupils have not grappled with the learning – they have just taken it in without question. In schools where pupils are docile in attitude, it is possible to teach like this; however, there is often an unpleasant surprise when results are received and some pupils have not done as well as expected. Their polite, biddable behaviour and compliance has covered up crucial misunderstandings and a lot of learning that was secure only at a surface level.

Finally, but importantly, teaching is a demanding and time-consuming profession. If we can do all we can to ensure the learning sticks during the initial teaching time, there will be much less need to increase our workload by replicating and repeating our lessons. Instead of running yet another revision session after school, we can use that valuable time to assess, feed back or plan more engaging and sticky lessons, so the learners engage and develop the tools to revise and secure learning for themselves.

Teaching is a career that is increasingly time pressured. This book provides a range of useful techniques designed to make learning and lessons as sticky as possible. You can just turn to these sections to receive a range of useful sticky, practical and pupil-tested classroom strategies in the Toolkit which forms the final two chapters of this book. These will enhance engagement and learning in any lesson. Your pupils will find that the learning sticks, and you will discover some new and engaging techniques nestling alongside others that you may have used before but be pleased to rediscover. However, some teachers will want to assure themselves of the research and background philosophy behind these strategies. For this reason, Chapters 1–9 cover the research philosophy and classroom realities behind the concept of sticky teaching and learning.

Research is important – after all, we don't want to fritter away time and energy on something that doesn't work or is just the latest in a line of teaching fads. However, each school is different. It has its own unique set of circumstances and contexts. Pupils and teachers within an individual school are also different. It is essential to be aware of this whenever we are seeking to improve and change our practice. On occasion, undigested research findings are trotted out as a panacea to cure all ills in a school. Unfortunately, it isn't as simple as that. I have briefly summarised some of the pertinent research in this book, but it is important that you think about this critically: the research implications must be appropriate to the context and needs of your pupils. Most of all, it is essential to be open-minded. If we are seeking to make specific improvements to the way we make learning sticky in our lessons, then we really need to trial new techniques, solicit feedback from pupils and ponder upon our findings for ourselves. For this to happen, there are 'thinking points' and suggested actions throughout the book to enable you to note down your thoughts and observations as you read – I do encourage you to do this.

I hope you enjoy *Sticky Teaching and Learning*. By reading and reflecting on these issues you will be well on the way to getting your pupils thinking and learning for themselves. Most importantly, you will be helping them learn how to make their learning stick and helping them develop crucial life skills – as well as obtaining the best set of examination results possible!

Most of all, relish it, try out the practical lesson ideas in the Toolkit with your students, in your school or college and talk to your pupils and fellow teachers to explore what is successful and has a real impact. Do let me know how you get on and what you find useful.

Caroline Bentley-Davies
www.bentley-davies.co.uk
Twitter: @realcbd

Contents

Introduction
What Is Sticky Teaching and Learning and Why Does It Matter?

 There is no learning without remembering.

Socrates (attrib.) ,,

Metacognition and sticky teaching

Sticky teaching means teaching in a way that makes learning memorable. It aims to maximise pupils' ability to remember, recall and respond to what we have taught them. One dictionary definition of sticky as 'long lasting' suggests that it is important for the learning to persist. The intention is to make the learning experience as engaging and adhesive as possible, so the pupils get immersed in what they are doing and can recall the key learning later. However, sticky teaching is about more than just trying to make learning experiences engaging and unforgettable.

An underlying principle of sticky teaching is that pupils should be engaged in the thinking processes involved in what they are learning. This encourages them to use metacognition (thinking about the thinking and learning process for themselves) so they can reflect on how they found the learning activity, what helped or hindered them and how they might do it differently next time. Research shows that pupils who practise and develop their metacognitive skills make much better progress than those who don't. The ability to reflect and then tweak and adapt our next approach to learning is crucial in becoming an effective and resilient learner. The Education

Endowment Foundation's Teaching and Learning Toolkit summarises the effectiveness and cost of a range of different strategies designed to raise pupil achievement.[1] It cites metacognition as a top educational strategy: if managed effectively, it has a huge impact on improving pupils' learning, equivalent to, on average, eight months of pupil progress. Moreover, it is also relatively low in cost to implement in schools – important in these financially straitened times. Given the strong research pedigree of this approach, it is vital that our pupils' metacognitive skills are developed as early and as effectively as possible.

Developing pupils' metacognitive skills is vital on many different levels. We know that if pupils receive a range of interactive and effective learning experiences, then it is likely that they will engage and be more interested in what they are doing. This will help them to better remember and recall the ideas, understanding and key concepts that you are teaching because they are incredibly involved in the lesson. However, it is the ability to self-evaluate and reflect on their success in learning that makes for the most independent and successful learners. The skill of self-reflection is crucial in developing resilience towards learning, which in turn allows pupils to stand back and reflect on their own performance and consider how things can be improved next time. Good metacognitive practice allows pupils to think about how they have performed and why this might have been. It helps them work out how their learning strategies could be refined and improved for the next occasion. This clearly leads to better learning and greater success. It is a virtuous cycle.

When we think about our own past learning experiences, we can see how an emphasis on metacognitive skills might have helped us to achieve better outcomes. When I was at school, being encouraged to develop better self-reflection would have really helped my learning, certainly in the subjects where I struggled. For example, I remember starting French lessons as an excited 11-year-old. My motivation was extremely high because I was to be learning a new language. However, I had no prior experience in

---

1   See https://educationendowmentfoundation.org.uk/evidence-summaries/teaching-learning-toolkit.

learning a language, so I had no previous strategies to draw on. Early on, I recall being given a long list of French vocabulary about different types of pets to learn over the weekend for a test on the following Monday. I started trying to memorise the list in a diligent fashion on the Sunday afternoon; however, I didn't do very well in the test, despite spending a lot of time staring at and rereading the words. I got the first word *lapin* quite effortlessly, *poisson rouge* (I remembered from previous colour vocabulary that *rouge* was red) but not many others. After the test and my poor results, I felt very disheartened. My excitement and motivation for learning French was fast disappearing. I had spent ages 'revising', but I still hadn't succeeded.

Did the teacher help us by discussing strategies to help us improve next time? No, she did not. Those of us who had gained fewer than half marks were told sternly that we would be retested in the next lesson – and woe betide us if we didn't improve. We know now that trying to cram in last-minute revision won't work as our working memory is soon overloaded.[2] We need to embed, revisit and review our learning across time to become successful learners. Although I had to study French up to GCSE, it is fair to say that I underachieved by at least one grade in the final examination. At no point in any of the lessons do I remember our teacher discussing different methods to help us learn vocabulary effectively. We weren't given a range of different techniques to experiment with and we certainly weren't encouraged to reflect after our tests on which revision and learning techniques worked for us and which didn't. This would have been so useful, not only in that specific test but for all vocabulary learning in French and a range of other subject areas. It would have allowed us, at a young age, to understand that there are different approaches for committing information to memory and that we could directly influence our own success by taking a particular approach to our revision.

---

2 See Centre for Education Statistics and Evaluation, *Cognitive Load Theory: Research That Teachers Really Need to Understand* (September 2017). Available at: https://www.cese.nsw.gov.au/publications-filter/cognitive-load-theory-research-that-teachers-really-need-to-understand.

importantly, we would have realised that we had control over our ...ning and that our failures weren't absolute. We could learn from them a..d do better next time. We should have been encouraged to be reflective, to think about how we would alter our strategies for the next time we were asked to learn a vocabulary list, write an essay or revise for an exam. Instead, we came to the quick realisation that a few classmates appeared to get top marks effortlessly and others didn't (no matter how long they stared at a sheet of words). As you can imagine, if you weren't a top scorer this was very demotivating. How immensely helpful it would have been to discuss tactics with each other: what revision techniques had we used? How successful or otherwise had we found them? What would we adapt for next time? It certainly would have helped to maintain learner enthusiasm and resilience, because if you were less successful in a test you would be encouraged to reflect on the reasons behind this. Could you have used a different technique to revise? Perhaps leaving all your revision to the morning of the test wasn't the best approach. Would making flashcards or listening to your speech recorded onto your phone help you? What technique did your partner use that helped them to improve their marks from the last test? What helped you to do better than your last test? You get the picture.

Building resilience is crucial for students. We certainly don't always succeed first time as adults, and nor should we. If we are setting ourselves appropriately challenging goals, there will undoubtedly be false starts and we will need to make amendments and adjustments to our approach. Resilience is important not just for passing tests but for building a successful life. Everybody faces setbacks, so it is necessary to have the right strategies to respond to them constructively. To create effective learners, it is essential that we help them to develop and hone these skills, and ultimately to own them for themselves. Across a student's total school experience, it is likely that they will sit 500 or more tests, assessments or examinations. A typical student will experience a minimum of one test or exam per school week (often many more!), even if it is just a quick spelling or maths test. If you are reading this book as an educator, you will have been at least moderately if not highly successful in passing tests, learning and all that it entails. But imagine for a moment that you weren't. How long after receiving repeatedly poor test marks would you have wanted to give up? If you didn't have successful strategies and the know-how to alter your approach to learning and feedback, then it is likely to have been very soon indeed.

The outlook isn't all smooth sailing for those brilliant 11-year-old test-takers either. Some students who start out as high achievers, who pass GCSE examinations with the minimum of effort, seem to struggle post 16. They find the challenging demands of A level or higher education an unpleasant shock. After all, they succeeded effortlessly in earlier years, so they have never had to grapple and find strategies to deal with these setbacks before. Consequently, these individuals often underachieve and lose motivation at these crucial stages in their education. The problem? They have not mastered how to struggle and strive without sinking. They have not learned how to review, adapt and adopt different strategies with their learning. They have previously found success without having to try all that hard. They have not developed resilience because they have not mastered metacognition or self-regulation (the ability to self-motivate). The implications for this are serious for these individuals, who may lose motivation and end up underachieving in school and in later life.

For the moment, flex those metacognitive muscles yourself and take time for a thinking point.

Thinking point

- When did you last learn something new that you found challenging?

- How did you feel about learning it?

- What strategies helped or hindered you? What motivated or demotivated you?

- In your lessons, do you discuss and give pupils examples of strategies to help them revise and consolidate their learning?

- Do you encourage pupils to reflect on, adapt and review their strategies and their effectiveness?

- Do you encourage pupils to share their successful approaches with each other?

- Do you explicitly discuss metacognition and its importance in improving learning with pupils?

- What do your pupils find effective in helping them to learn and secure new learning?

- What topics or concepts might they need more help with to make the learning stick?

What this book will do for you

This book will guide you through some teaching methods and practical strategies to develop more resilient and effective learners and, most importantly, it will help to ensure that what you teach really sticks. Chapters 1 to 9 explain and unpick the key aspects of teaching that contribute to effective long-term learning. By examining the crucial roles that teacher expectation and pupil mindset play in developing resilient learners, we will explore how you can influence pupil effort and improve outcomes. Chapter 1 discusses how to foster the attitudes and skills that make this possible. This is developed in Chapter 2, which considers the significance of the classroom climate in encouraging learner independence and examines the impact of the emotional and physical environment on promoting individual competence and self-reliance. The importance of planning as a foundation to great long-term retention is reviewed in Chapter 3, first by looking at the planning of individual lessons and then highlighting some common pitfalls. The impact of retrieval practice in planning is considered in Chapter 4, and we look at how to improve memory and performance. Chapter 5 underlines the consequence of this in a case study from a real GCSE revision class. Chapters 6 to 9 examine various teaching approaches for developing pupils' understanding and knowledge and how to make these more effective in retaining learning. These are linked to questioning and feedback in its various forms: the skills of questioning in Chapter 6, why we need to engage with getting things wrong in Chapter 7, the impact of effective feedback on learning in Chapter 8, and the power of peer and self-assessment in Chapter 9.

In the Toolkit, you will find 50 engaging and tried-and-tested teaching techniques that will enthuse and inspire your pupils to first think carefully and to engage with and embed learning. The Toolkit is divided up between classroom teaching techniques, which will help to make learning stick, and quick plenary ideas to help check on the success of this. They are all designed for maximum participation so there are no passengers sitting it out on the sidelines. This is a crucial part of the success of the sticky teaching approach. These activities are all underpinned by Bjork's maxim of 'desirable difficulty' – that making the learning and reviewing challenging is critical to ensuring retention.[3] Finally, there is a bibliography, because this is a book for the busy classroom teacher and therefore touches only lightly on the research.

---

3   Elizabeth L. Bjork and Robert Bjork, Making Things Hard on Yourself, But in a Good Way: Creating Desirable Difficulty to Enhance Learning. In Morton Gernsbacher, Richard Pew, Leaette Hough and James Pomerantz (eds), *Psychology and the Real World: Essays Illustrating Fundamental Contributions to Society* (New York: Worth, 2009), pp. 56–64.

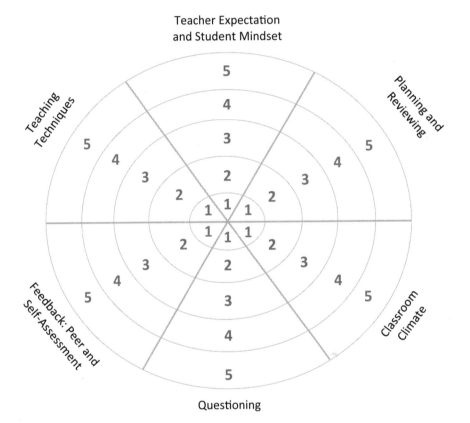

Teacher Expectation
and Student Mindset

Teaching
Techniques

Planning and
Reviewing

Feedback: Peer and
Self-Assessment

Classroom
Climate

Questioning

The wheel of sticky teaching

Chapter 1
The Sticky Classroom: Teacher Expectations and Student Mindsets

 When we take people ... merely as they are, we make them worse; when we treat them as if they were what they should be, we improve them as far as they can be improved.

Johann Wolfgang von Goethe, tr. Thomas Carlyle,
Wilhelm Meister's Apprenticeship and Travels

The six areas of sticky teaching

To make learning stick successfully there are six important areas that must work together effectively: teacher expectation and student mindset, planning and reviewing, classroom climate, questioning, feedback (peer and self-assessment) and teaching techniques. The wheel of sticky teaching on page 8 shows these six key areas.[1]

The bands within the circle are labelled from 1 to 5, with 5 being the zone of most effective or confident practice and 1 the zone of least proficiency. Use the wheel as a self-reflection tool to evaluate how effectively you feel you are working in each area. For example, in the *classroom climate* segment, a score of 5 would indicate that this area is operating brilliantly: the students are taking responsibility for developing aspects of their own learning, they

---

1   An electronic copy of the wheel can be accessed from my website: www. bentley-davies.co.uk.

are skilled at self-reviewing their work and they are effective independent learners. The classroom and the physical environment would also strongly support this. In contrast, a score of 1 would indicate that the students are overly dependent on the teacher and that they might resist being asked to think for themselves. The resources in the classroom to support this area would also underdeveloped.

Have a look at the wheel and think about where you might be currently for each of these areas. Of course, it isn't the specific number that matters, but the reflection about each area that it encourages. We will be considering each of the six areas in detail, so if you feel one area is less developed than the others, then the specific chapter related to it will help you to find strategies to boost your score. Clearly, the six segments of the wheel are interconnected – learning won't be successfully sticky if you spend all your energy on one segment to the detriment of the others. This is because they impact on each other, as we shall see when we discuss each segment of the wheel and unpick what success looks like for each individual area.

Teacher expectations for effective sticky learning

As we unpack this a little more, you will see that *teacher expectation and student mindset* is right at the top of the wheel. This is because both are crucial in making learning stick. Pupils take their lead from the teacher, and there are countless ways that they can tell whether or not you believe in them. Pupils can spot whether you think they will complete a task to the best of their ability – if you think they have the skills to succeed – or whether, if they push back and behave in a resistant way, you might just give in and let them off that learning activity by providing the answers for them or accepting their below par efforts. Pupils often test you. They know that if they are 'difficult' or reluctant, you are less likely to force them to complete challenging tasks. They know they can get away with more and this will mean an easier time for them in lessons.

As a teacher, the temptation to take the path of least resistance can be quite strong. The urge to just lecture pupils, to tell them what they need to do to pass the examination, can be attractive. There are fewer battles to win because we aren't making them think for themselves. We might appear to be 'covering' the required curriculum much more quickly and making much faster progress across the programme of study. This is very often deceptive. It is only when the learning is reviewed or we consider assessment outcomes that we realise this learning has only been operating at a surface level. It hasn't really stuck.

We might well have a raft of engaging teaching techniques at our fingertips, but if we don't have high enough expectations of our pupils then the quality of the learning is doomed. High expectations are essential. Pupils need to know that we anticipate maximum achievement from them: they will be expected to be actively involved in their learning and to revisit and learn from their mistakes. All this really matters in making the quality of the learning good and making it stick.

High expectations are demonstrated by the type of tasks set by the teacher and how they are organised. Are the tasks sufficiently demanding and challenging for *all* pupils? There can sometimes be a tendency to give tasks with too little challenge to those with more limited ability in that area or who have special educational needs. Tasks must be tailored to the abilities of the pupils; however, all tasks need to push and challenge all pupils appropriately, even those who find the subject area difficult. They still need to be appropriately challenged and taken out of their comfort zone. All learners, regardless of their starting points, should find that the tasks stretch them and move them on with their learning so they make really good progress.

I observed a teacher who was known to achieve exceptional outcomes for pupils of all abilities. In her lessons I noticed how the language she used communicated these expectations. She urged her pupils to 'think like geographers'. There was an almost tangible air of high expectation and excitement about what they were learning. When they were organising their work, she encouraged them to plan out carefully which geographical terms they would use (checking them carefully), so they were 'writing like geographers'. Initially, I thought this was an extremely high ability class, particularly as the exemplar work she showed them was very accomplished. However, the exemplar was used to help them deconstruct and understand what was successful about it. They were encouraged to think about how to take their work to the best level possible.

This was a class with many pupils who were not of high ability and who struggled to make progress or remain motivated in other lessons. However, here they were motivated by their learning because of the teacher's evident belief in them, combined with how carefully she set up the learning to support and challenge them. Of course, it is no good just telling students to 'think like geographers' if you don't demonstrate what this would look like in practice and actually support them to help them work towards it. Their eventual outcomes were so much higher than their results in other subjects because of this approach of high expectations coupled with effective guidance and support.

It is interesting to compare this successful approach to the attitude of a maths teacher who made a telling throwaway comment to a class of borderline 4/5 GCSE pupils. Discussing the intricacies of a topic, he made a very telling remark to the class, stating: 'Most of you should have the intelligence to get this ...' Ouch. No wonder many of these pupils were lacking in motivation and doubted their abilities. It is obvious to pupils which of their teachers believe they will be successful learners, and teach them accordingly, and which ones don't. Pupils' efforts and behaviour reflect and magnify the expectations of their teachers. This is borne out by the phenomenon of the Pygmalion effect: when researchers Robert Rosenthal and Lenore Jacobson told teachers that some of their pupils were very high achievers and would make incredible progress over the year, this is what happened, even though the specific pupils had in fact been selected at random.[2] The combined effect of the teacher's positive response and

---

2 Robert Rosenthal and Lenore Jacobson, Pygmalion in the Classroom, *Urban Review*, 3 (1968): 16–20.

expectation of great achievement and the attention they focused on helping those 'gifted' pupils to achieve success was that they thrived and made exceptional progress.[3] Unfortunately, the reverse is also true: if a previous class teacher tells you that a particular pupil is poorly behaved or puts in minimum effort, it is likely that you will be watching out for evidence that confirms this information. This is called the Golem effect. Starting the year and the lesson afresh and telling the class that you have high expectations of them all is a positive and practical way to set up a good learning atmosphere.

How are high expectations signalled to pupils?

As the previous examples illustrate, the language you use as a teacher is key in signalling your high expectations to pupils. Explaining that something is a 'challenge' but that they have the skills to master it is vastly different from telling them that they might find something 'too hard'. The success of our communication is also deeply influenced by our tone of voice and body language. Do we sound excited and upbeat about the learning? Do we present tasks in a firm, clear and no-nonsense way so that pupils know we are purposeful and mean business? Are we crystal clear about the success criteria so pupils know what they are aiming for? By combining these areas skilfully we communicate our high expectations for our pupils.

---

3 Bradley Busch, Great Expectations: How to Help Your Students Fulfil Their Potential, *The Guardian* (31 August 2016). Available at: https://www.theguardian.com/teacher-network/2016/aug/31/great-expectations-how-to-help-your-students-fulfil-their-potential.

Student mindset: securing sticky learning

 Nothing in the world can take the place of persistence.

Calvin Coolidge

The student mindset is equally as important as that of the teacher. It is the student who needs to master the material and become a successful learner. Of course, for students to maximise their potential and develop their skills to the highest level, it is crucial that they have the right attitude or mindset. When we talk about the need for learning to be sticky, there is an inherent challenge in it. Some students are much better at learning, regardless of the quality of the teaching. However, *all* students will find some aspects of a subject hard to master. For the student who does not find a subject easy or does not enjoy a topic, getting the learning to stick in their memory is a big ask, which is why the mindset of our learners is so significant.

The idea of the student mindset incorporates many of the important messages from the research into growth mindset pioneered by US academic Carol Dweck in her book *Mindset: The New Psychology of Success*. Essentially, for students to grow and develop their skills they need to be willing to adopt a growth mindset towards their learning and interactions with others. Dweck studied different children's responses to being faced with a difficult challenge. Those who had a growth mindset were not daunted or put off when success did not come easily. Instead, when they found something particularly hard or got things wrong, they saw this as a learning opportunity and a chance to grow and develop further. The children who thrived when they were given a challenging task to complete had a specific attitude. Rather than believing that these tasks were beyond their grasp, they rose to the challenge and, what is more, found motivation in the very fact that it was hard to accomplish. One child who persevered said: 'It's a lot more difficult for me than I thought it would be, but it's what I want to do, so that only makes me more determined. When they tell me I can't, it really gets me going.'[4]

Dweck's research highlights the power of a growth mindset in students (and teachers) in helping them to make exceptional progress with their learning. This is because they don't accept defeat when learning is a real struggle – instead, they welcome and relish the struggle. They see mistakes and failure as temporary, and not as something demotivating. However, Dweck also highlights how some individuals have a very fixed mindset and how extremely limiting this can be. This is because it puts a barrier on learning and development. A fixed mindset is essentially believing that our intelligence and ability are predefined: they are set and there isn't a great deal we can do to improve them. If our abilities are fixed, we are therefore either limited or lucky in what we have and how far we can progress in our learning. This is encapsulated in the statements that you sometimes hear people say, such as, 'I just can't do maths' or 'I've always been hopeless at sport.'

It seems clear that educators should have a growth mindset themselves and should foster one in their students so they can strive to improve their skills. However, the presence of a fixed mindset can sometimes be quite subtle, but none the less dangerous for that. It is the teacher who decides not to ask Fatima that question because she thinks it might be slightly too hard for her, or who doesn't encourage Ethan to work outside of his comfort zone by persuading him to lead in the group discussion because initially he won't enjoy it. It is the teaching assistant who decides it would be kinder to Tomas not to push him too much because he finds maths a challenge. Although these examples of a fixed mindset are often kindly intentioned, their impact can have disastrous implications for students, their future efforts and progress in learning.

One personal example illustrates how a kindly but ultimately limiting fixed mindset comment can hinder a pupil's progress. For much of my school

---

4   Carol S. Dweck, *Mindset: The New Psychology of Success* (New York: Ballantine, 2007), p. 23.

career, I hovered in the lower end of the top set for German. I was keen to do well and wanted to push myself and improve. However, I remember answering a certain question in a German lesson: I started responding and tried to develop my answer so that it had more detail. My teacher responded by saying, 'You've got the first bit right. You'd be better off quitting while you're ahead.' I shrivelled back into my shell. I had been given a clear message: only answer if you are 100% sure it is correct. You might wonder, quite rightly, what is the point of that? Where is the learning or development? Of course, great teachers should encourage risk-taking and see mistakes as temporary detours on the path towards the right answer. Sometimes teachers can lower their expectations of certain classes or individuals. They don't want pupils taking risks.

Having a learning ambition was not encouraged by my teacher – only a faultless answer was acceptable. From then on, I only answered questions when I was very sure that I would give a 100% correct response. As a consequence, lots of learning opportunities were lost. Firstly, if the teacher had congratulated me for taking a risk and trying, then I (and the rest of the class) would have been much more willing to respond to questions in the future. Greater participation in the questioning sessions in the lesson would have given the teacher better feedback about the misconceptions in our understanding of key concepts. Furthermore, allowing another member of the class to rework my answer so that it was correct would have helped me to see where I had gone wrong and how to improve. But, most of all, the teacher could have encouraged me to learn from my error and to think about how I could get it right next time. How could I fix the correct answer in my memory for next time?

Having a fixed mindset, whether as a child or teacher, limits achievement. If pupils feel afraid of failure and believe they must always get everything right, they can become unwilling to try and fail. This can lead to them not challenging themselves to try out an answer or self-selecting easier tasks or subjects so they never get anything wrong, which also means that they don't benefit from correction by others. They may be unwilling to grapple, redraft, reconsider or improve work because they are seeking a 'perfect' exercise book and want to make it look like their learning is effortless. Struggling and getting things wrong undermines their view of themselves. This is especially true if teachers and their peers only reward perfection rather than continuous effort and improvement. Of course, we know that to really maximise potential and secure learning we have to push ourselves. Accepting failure as a first attempt is fine – it should be welcomed. Perhaps failure should be redefined as a first try or attempt at learning. After all, if pupils are getting everything effortlessly correct, then they are not being challenged sufficiently or reaching their full potential. The hugely successful J. K. Rowling reminds us that 'some failure in life is inevitable. It is impossible to live without failing at something, unless you live so cautiously that you might as well have not lived at all – in which case, you fail by default.'[5]

In her work on mindset, Dweck talks of the power of 'not yet' – the idea that in fulfilling our potential we might stumble or make a misstep. This is fine: if we get something wrong it is because we have not got it *yet*. The idea of *yet* shows future possibilities. It is massively powerful in motivating pupils and helping them to realise that although they have not mastered it *yet*, it is still within their reach with sufficient effort, reflection and suitable strategies about how to move past obstacles.

The importance of a growth mindset is that it helps pupils to learn that there are things they can do to help them improve. They can take control of their learning and it can be made to stick. Their intelligence isn't fixed and they, in Dweck's words, can 'take charge of the processes that bring success'.[6] This means pupils seizing the opportunity to reflect on their work, learning from their errors, taking steps to make corrections and thinking about how they will improve their approach for next time. However, if they have a fixed mindset they will have a set view of their ability and their results will confirm this. They will want to get everything right first time and they may

5   Joanne K. Rowling, The Fringe Benefits of Failure and the Importance of Imagination. Harvard University commencement address, 5 June 2008. Available at: https://news.harvard.edu/gazette/story/2008/06/text-of-j-k-rowling-speech.
6   Dweck, *Mindset*, p. 101.

have a crisis of confidence if they make mistakes. They are keen to confirm their intelligence, so any errors throw this view of themselves into doubt. Since they feel they are not in charge of their own learning, their resilience is hampered when they suffer setbacks. A poor grade makes a child with a fixed mindset feel stupid or look for external excuses (e.g. 'I had too many tests on that week' or 'It was too noisy in the test room'), rather than tackle the issue head-on and think what they will learn from the experience that will lead to improvements in their learning next time.

If we want learning to stick, it is important for teachers to help their pupils develop a growth mindset and to utilise this in the way they teach.

Thinking point

- How do the lesson activities you choose highlight your high expectations for all pupils?

- What do you do so your pupils know you have the highest expectations for all of them?

- How do you encourage pupils to develop high expectations of themselves and their learning?

- What words and phrases do you use to motivate and communicate your expectations to your class?

- How do you communicate to pupils that it is desirable to reflect and try again, that they are not expected to achieve everything successfully the first time?

- How do you react when pupils make mistakes?

- Do you model the growth mindset approach in the way you approach your teaching by acknowledging that it is desirable to learn from your mistakes?

Chapter 2
The Classroom Climate for Sticky Learning: Increasing Pupil Independence

 Spoon feeding in the long run teaches us nothing but the shape of the spoon.

E. M. Forster

What might you expect to see in a sticky classroom?

Having an effective classroom climate is important in promoting pupils' independence and in making learning stick. Climate can refer to two different but interconnected areas. Firstly, the physical environment – the space where learning takes place. What does it look and feel like to be a learner in this area? How does the climate help or hinder the pupils? What resources are available? How are pupils encouraged to use them effectively to gain independence and assist their learning?

Secondly, but no less importantly, how do the adults and other learners in the room create a tangible learning climate? How do they encourage pupils to become more independent with their learning so they are not over-reliant on their teacher? How do they promote pupils to think for themselves? How do they ensure that all pupils participate? It is worth thinking about what this looks like in action.

I observe many lessons and see a wide range of approaches. In many lessons, pupils are developing effective skills that will promote their independence. Interestingly, while you might imagine that older students would be more independent than younger pupils, this does not always seem to be the case. It is frequently younger pupils who most readily take on board the steps needed to become self-sufficient. I recall a friend telling me that she had been to visit the current Year 6 pupils at a feeder primary school and was incredibly impressed with their approach. They ran pupil councils, set up buddy systems with younger pupils to develop reading and were very self-reliant in their lessons. They were skilled at peer working and gave effective feedback to each other. The primary school had really fostered a sense of impressive independence. Imagine her surprise when teaching some of the same pupils at the start of Year 7, when they raised their hands to ask what to do because they had finished writing on the page – should they turn over? The amazingly confident and independent Year 6 pupils had become dependent Year 7s who were nervous about doing the 'wrong' thing in their new school.

However, it is in our power as teachers to create an atmosphere conducive to promoting pupil independence. Great learning becomes a partnership between the teacher and the pupils when pupils are secure about developing and taking some responsibility for their own learning. The teacher is the educational expert, of course, but it is those pupils who really get involved in their learning who flourish.

Two classroom climates

The following examples show two snapshots of different lessons where the independence of pupils is very contrasting. Have a read and reflect on the issues raised in them.

Classroom 1

Pupils (primary aged) are well practised in several effective learning routines – for example, individuals in the group have assigned roles and responsibilities, they distribute equipment purposefully at the start of a lesson, they listen attentively to the teacher's explanations and when she asks, 'What questions do you have?' they feel confident and secure enough to ask for elaboration and further information. Instead of directly answering these questions herself, the teacher first asks if any of the other pupils can provide the answer and allows the other pupils the opportunity to address them. She then makes any necessary clarifications to ensure that all the pupils have a clear understanding of what they need to do next.

The pupils work purposefully on independent work and make use of several areas of the classroom. There is an 'enable table' at one side of the room, which has various equipment and useful information relating to the subject or topic they are studying. For example, in mathematics there might be various pieces of equipment to help and enable them to work out answers and solve problems. The pupils feel confident that they can select and use appropriate equipment to assist them with their learning without having to ask their teacher first.

The classroom walls have engaging displays that are used by the children to check their work or inspire them. For example, a science display has much of the key vocabulary for the topic they are studying linked to helpful visual diagrams with definitions. Another display gives five strategies for writing the opening of a story and lists some useful sentence stems as starters. There is also a large checklist with questions to help pupils reflect on and check their work for themselves. Pupils can be seen referring to these displays and checking their work, rather than immediately asking the teacher for help.

Pupils have 'peer partners' who work with them to check each other's work. This peer assessment strongly contributes towards securing their learning. This is because the pupils get the opportunity to talk through the decisions they have made with another pupil of a similar ability. They make suitable amendments and improvements to their work before the teacher views it.

Pupils look over assessed work carefully and make corrections. They record key words and corrections in the back of their books. They refer to them, making use of their amendments so they learn how to improve. The children regularly spend 10 minutes at the end of a lesson testing each other on their spelling and key words. They check that they have secured the correct knowledge and learned from their mistakes.

The teaching assistant sits with a specific group of children (this rotates depending on the pupils' needs). Some learners within the group complain that they are 'stuck'. She can be heard asking probing questions that get the children to think about what they can do next to get themselves 'unstuck'. There is a pleasant atmosphere of positive productivity and the pupils can be heard discussing and checking their learning with one another. The pupils listen carefully when their peers give responses to questions, add to their answers and make thoughtful reflections.

Classroom 2

The students are very dependent on the teacher, who is trying to give out equipment and explain tasks simultaneously. The room has no helpful displays and there are no resources easily available for students to self-check aspects of their work. All the guidance and checking guidance comes directly from the teacher; it is not co-constructed with the students. The students don't have confidence in their own understanding or decision-making. When they finish their work they immediately clamour for the teacher or teaching assistant to check it for them. Their responses when the teacher gives them feedback show that they are only hungry for praise, and see task completion rather than securing learning as the desired result.

Thinking point

- Which aspects of either classroom do you recognise?

- Which parts of Classroom 1's climate do you think is the most important for developing pupils' independence?

- Are there any elements of your classroom climate that you would like to develop further with your own classes?

- Is there another teacher in the school that you think maintains an excellent climate for independence? Could you arrange to visit their lesson or discuss their strategies with them?

Why the right climate supports great learning

The inspirational teacher-educator Ron Berger talks at length about great learning requiring teachers to model 'an ethic of excellence in maintaining physical facilities and in developing a climate of physical and emotional safety for all students'.[1]

The physical environment gives our students lots of information about our expectations for them, and how seriously we take the business of teaching and learning. A well-equipped and well-organised classroom models the type of behaviour we hope to see from them. A classroom where students can select from well-managed resources gives them not just the impression that they matter, but also the practical means to check their work or find the tools they need to enhance it.

---

1 Ron Berger, *An Ethic of Excellence: Building a Culture of Craftsmanship with Students* (Portsmouth, NH: Heinemann, 2003), p. 150.

I once conducted a review where one of the areas the school was concerned about was the poverty of students' expression and their limited vocabulary. However, observing lesson after lesson, it was evident that although the teachers tried to encourage students to improve their word choice, it really wasn't happening. When they asked them to give different word choices, the teachers were met with blank stares and shrugs. The students didn't have access to thesauruses to find alternative words or dictionaries to check the meanings of their peers' suggestions. Walls and displays offered no support or encouragement in this area.

The extremely limited word choices used by their peers were recycled constantly in lessons, with only a small amount of new vocabulary being suggested. The only person adding to the students' repertoire of new vocabulary was the teacher, and sometimes even she struggled to come up with good lexical alternatives when placed on the spot. When some students offered a word choice whose meaning wasn't quite appropriate to the context, there was no mechanism to get them to check the meaning of the word for themselves. Instead, the teacher had to correct them, thereby extending the gap between expert teacher and novice student and, importantly, increasing the dependency of the student on the teacher as the fount of all knowledge.

The judicious use of resources, both physical and online, can empower students to check things for themselves. This teaches them a valuable lesson since it shows them they have the capability to find out things independently. They do not need to automatically defer to the teacher. We have all experienced the situation where 20 students all want their work to be checked *now* – it is exhausting, stressful and physically impossible! Getting students into the habit of self-reliance is important, as we want them to have the ability to check and expand their own knowledge. They need to be able to carry on learning so they can do this when we aren't there – whether that is at home completing self-study, in the examination hall or later in higher education or the world of work.

While observing an English lesson in another school, I watched on as a teacher struggled momentarily to correctly spell 'onomatopoeia' on the board. (It is a word that can intimidate even the most accomplished of spellers, especially when you are being observed!) While she was hesitating, one boy called out: 'Miss, shall I just look it up for you?' She gladly accepted and he swiftly referred to the dictionary on his desk and confirmed the correct spelling with her. Although initially she appeared embarrassed, she took five minutes with the class to discuss the issue. Admitting that she found it a tricky word, she asked the pupils to spend a few minutes with their neighbour thinking about how they could master the spelling of such an awkward word in a way that they would remember. Then she asked several pairs to share their approaches. These included some really interesting ones, from those you might expect – finding a word within a word (ono-*mat*-opoeia) – to the fact that some of them had learned how to spell it by learning a song to the tune of 'Old MacDonald Had a Farm' with their previous teacher!

Pausing the lesson to create a meaningful discussion about strategies to remember the spelling of a tricky word and sharing this with the class shows metacognition in action. She demonstrated that even as a qualified teacher, she needed to find new approaches to remind herself how to spell difficult words and to make the correct spelling stick! It is very valuable for teachers to model how to be an effective lifelong learner. Of course, as teachers we need to keep our subject knowledge sharp, but we all have those moments when our memory lapses or we make a silly error. Modelling how to deal with this and showing how to embed learning is an extremely helpful approach to adopt. Students can learn so much from this approach if it is demonstrated by the teacher and then if they are given the opportunity to practise it. It is much preferable to the attitude of a science teacher I once observed who, when a very able Year 10 student correctly queried his spelling of a key scientific term, snapped back, 'This isn't an English lesson – spelling isn't important!'

Modelling and talking through our responses in order to deeply embed learning enables students to see reflection in action. Having mini thinking 'pit stops' in the lesson helps students to realise that they need to actively find strategies to help secure tricky learning for themselves – it won't just happen automatically. We all must struggle and strive to make learning stick.

The physical climate: wall displays

Wall displays can be used in a variety of ways to reinforce learning and to help make key information stick. The research on the impact of displays in improving learning is slim and, for this reason, some schools justify a no-display policy. This is a great shame: when I have visited schools where room after room, corridor after corridor is just a bland backdrop of grey-painted breeze blocks my heart sinks. You can't tell if you are in the geography block or the science department. It seems a missed opportunity not to be celebrating the best work in that area, promoting the subject and enhancing students' learning. In other classrooms, the displays appear to be simply an attractive backdrop to the learning, and may, in fact, have so much going on in the form of busy colours and assorted materials that it is rather distracting for the students trying to concentrate on the learning in the lesson.

However, I have observed countless lessons where a well-planned and well-used display really helps to reinforce the learning and promotes independence. This includes:

- Students selecting tasks from a 'challenge envelope' fixed to the wall once they have finished their work. Of course, the challenge needs to be a higher order task that brings together some of their previous learning; otherwise it simply becomes more of the same, which is anything but motivating.

- Examples of annotated work at different levels – helpfully illustrating to students what they need to be able to show in order to get to the next step. Even if these are just blown-up photocopies of introductions to essays, marked up to explain why they are effective, these can be useful for showing students what makes a quality piece of work and how to improve.

- A range of exciting ways to reinforce and embed key technical terms, such as matching the words and their meaning to visual images or to definitions displayed on the wall. If these are referred to and used in lessons by both teacher and students, they can help to embed learning.

- Exemplifications of different ways to start essays or longer answers, including sentence starters and connectives.

- Stimulating diagrams to visually represent key pieces of learning in different ways – for example, transforming a piece of text into a diagram, or vice versa.

- Collages or visual displays made by the students that synthesise information about key revision areas. These can be displayed for the rest of the class to refer to after the presentation.

- Checklists and key reminders about what students should be looking at when reviewing their work (with examples).

- In the news – a display that encourages students to bring in news articles related to the subject they are studying that can be explored in lessons. Students are more likely to be interested in a topic if they feel connected to it.

- Stages to greatness board – a display showing great quality work to 'give them a vision of their goal', as Ron Berger calls it.[2] Presenting a range of excellent work – with drafts demonstrating how they progressed over time – is both inspiring and instructive.

---

2 Berger, *An Ethic of Excellence*, p. 83.

The learning climate in the lesson: promoting independence

 Your teacher can open the door, but you must enter by yourself.

Chinese proverb

The learning climate in a lesson is best described as what it feels like to be in the lesson emotionally. How does the teacher (and any support staff) keep the children motivated, engaged and inspired to give their best? It can feel quite challenging to describe the learning climate – but although it might seem intangible, the results are not. It is the means through which the adults create a positive atmosphere conducive to effective learning.

Below are some questions to consider when creating a positive learning climate designed to help make learning stick successfully.

Is it safe for pupils to make mistakes and errors?

We want pupils to strive for success, so developing an unthreatening atmosphere in the learning environment is essential. Pupils need to feel safe in the lesson so they can have a go at trying challenging tasks and know that they can make mistakes without a loss of face. A teacher who encourages their pupils and welcomes mistakes will help them to achieve more challenging tasks than the teacher who sees a pupil's misstep as a slur on their own teaching. If we are encouraging our pupils to try appropriately challenging work, they will inevitably get some things wrong. This is a sign that they are pushing themselves and trying to work outside of their comfort zone, and therefore should be welcomed and encouraged.

Do you foster a risk-taking approach in your own teaching practice?

A good teacher should try out fresh and challenging approaches, thereby adding to their teaching repertoire. Simply put, we need to practise what we preach. For learning to stick successfully we might need to try a different approach to teaching a topic. This may well demand more of us as a teacher as it might require new methods, different resources or novel ways of explaining a task. We need to make sure that we are open to different ways of doing things before we can expect this flexibility and resilience from our pupils.

Do you feel you need to know everything?

As we have seen, a good teacher needs to role model being an effective learner. It is important to have handy strategies to deal with the unexpected, with the challenging question, with the mistake you made when you modelled a sample answer. However, if your Year 3 pupils are really excited about the topic of space, they might well ask you some thought-provoking questions to which you don't know the answers. In fact, the answers might not be known even by top astrophysicists! Encouraging pupils' interest to flourish without shutting down their excitement is key.

Of course, we all need to keep our subject knowledge fresh and look for novel approaches when teaching topics, but we can't always know everything about a subject. Having strategies to deal with the unexpected question is essential, whether it is adding the query to a question wall that displays pupils' questions related to a topic or suggesting that the children revisit the question in their homework and then feed back their answers in the next lesson. A question wall works well and makes for a display that is both inspiring and useful. It can be made interactive by progressing the questions along the board once the answers have been found. The answers can also be displayed, which will show the pupils how they have progressed, and it can also be referred to by pupils to consolidate their learning.

Do you learn with the pupils and make this clear?

A great deal of the enjoyment in teaching is discovering and responding to your pupils' insights and observations. Sometimes they will share ideas about poetry, art or approaches to tasks that make you think about something in a totally different way, even if you have taught it many times before. This is part of the sheer joy of teaching. Celebrate these moments and share what new insights you have found or discovered with your pupils.

If you find a memorable way to remember something, such as a mnemonic, then sharing it with the class will help them to realise that you too need to think consciously about the learning in the lesson. Likewise, if you sometimes make a mistake with something or find a technique tricky, share this with your class so that you can discuss strategies to overcome it. This is important because, as a pupil, it can sometimes be very disheartening if teachers make it look like everything is completely effortless. Talking through how you need to be careful not to forget the apostrophe or reflecting on how you nearly forgot to add the unit to your final calculation is a good reminder that accuracy in learning takes conscious effort and reflection.

Do pupils mini teach each other or the class?

Reciprocal teaching – whereby pupils teach each other aspects of the curriculum to consolidate their learning – has tangible benefits for both peer teacher and fellow pupil alike. John Hattie's assimilation of a wealth of educational research gives peer tutoring an effect size of 0.55. This is well into the zone of high effect on pupil progress. He also makes this comment: 'When students become the teachers of others, they learn as much as those they are teaching.'[3] Clearly, there are implications for how to go about this in practice, but getting peer partners to recap key ideas or explain them to each other – or even to the whole class or group – is evidently valuable.

Moreover, as we all know when called on to feed back training from an event to others in our school, having to accurately select and teach someone else the salient parts of a topic really challenges you to ensure that you understand them. It truly focuses the mind. As teachers, observing our pupils teaching on another can give us a clear insight into how effectively they have mastered an area or topic and what might need to be retaught in a more effective way. What could be more independent?

Do you encourage pupils to use strategies before they ask for help?

Whether it is the 'brain, book, buddy, boss' approach favoured by Jim Smith in his book *The Lazy Teacher's Handbook*,[4] or any similar such approach, strategies that help pupils to pause and think for themselves, ask others or check things before pouncing on you as the teacher are to be welcomed. Many pupils struggled to work independently through the straightforward home-schooling tasks their teachers had set for them during the first COVID-19 lockdown. There were various reasons, but the main one, as one teacher commented to me, was: 'They just couldn't follow simple instructions and – instead of scrolling down the page or doing as requested – had to get confirmation for even the simplest things by emailing the teacher to check.' After receiving hundreds of emails each day from her pupils, she admitted that it was just like the classroom conversations she had been having with them when they didn't read things through properly at the outset. Getting pupils used to checking and thinking for themselves first

---

3   John Hattie, *Visible Learning: A Synthesis of Over 800 Meta-Analyses Relating to Achievement* (Abingdon and New York: Routledge, 2009), p. 187.
4   Jim Smith, *The Lazy Teacher's Handbook – New Edition: How Your Students Learn More When You Teach Less* (Carmarthen: Independent Thinking Press, 2017).

isn't a quick fix – like any new habit it takes a lot of practice – but the rewards are immense.

Do the demands of the task challenge each pupil appropriately?

Even in a group that is strictly set by ability, not all pupils will be at the same stage in their learning. Each pupil brings different experiences and has different strengths across the curriculum. Some need greater guidance and coaching than others. Some very able pupils lack confidence in their great ideas, while others overestimate their abilities. Knowing your pupils well so that you can guide, coach and encourage them to give their best is vital. You can't personalise lessons for each pupil, of course – it would be madness to think you could have 30 different mini lessons happening simultaneously – but you can get to know them as individuals rather than as Class 3D. Learn what motivates them and how best to support them to flourish. Think about how to tweak tasks to add extra challenge for some pupils or provide helpful scaffolding for others. Consider also how to present tasks to inspire the confident learner and reassure the nervous one, so they both step up to the challenge. Ensuring that tasks are sufficiently demanding, but not alarm inducing, means they will be able to tackle them with enough self-confidence to make really good progress.

Do you allow pupils time to review their learning, both individually and, when appropriate, with suitable peers?

Those learners who develop the ability to check, review and self-correct their own work are at an immense advantage compared to those who over-rely on their teacher to do this for them. It is hard to carve out time in busy lessons to make this happen, but the rewards make it incredibly worthwhile. Getting pupils confident in working with peer buddies of a similar ability is very useful in helping them to reflect on their work and what they need to do to improve it. (Guidance on successfully managing peer and self-assessment can be found in Chapter 9.)

Do you receive feedback from the pupils about what is great about your classroom climate for independence and what could be better?

If you were to self-assess the classroom climate in your lessons, what would you say? Do you feel you have effective strategies to help pupils become more independent in their learning? Do you feel that over time the pupils' learning is progressing and they are becoming more independent? Importantly, do you feel that the pupils would say the same? This is the key question, because it is when we request and then act on feedback from our pupils that genuine improvements are achieved. As Hattie says: 'Feedback is most powerful when it is from student to the teacher.'[5] We will explore this much more in the next chapter.

---

5   Hattie, *Visible Learning*, p. 173.

Chapter 3
Sticky Stages in Teaching and Learning: Sticky Planning

 Plans are worthless, but planning is everything.

Dwight D. Eisenhower "

There are several steps to making learning both sticky and successful. Firstly, we need to think about planning. Good planning comes from the high expectations we set for our pupils. We need to plan appropriately challenging expectations for our pupils. There are several key things to think about in our planning that will really help us teach great lessons that stick.

What is the most important learning in this lesson or series of lessons?

The first question to consider is what exactly you want the pupils to learn or what skill you want them to develop in this lesson or series of lessons. This is of primary importance. Although you might have a range of exciting teaching strategies that you are itching to use, it is essential to start with the learning objective; otherwise, you might teach an engaging and interesting lesson but it might not further the pupils' learning. Stripping back planning to first thinking about the learning objective is crucial here. It is also essential to distinguish between the actions you want the pupils to undertake, the learning taking place and how you intend to make it stick. The following example shows why this is so important.

I was recently discussing with a newly qualified English teacher a lesson what she was planning. With regard to the learning objective for the lesson, she replied that she just wanted to 'get through and make progress on the next act of *Macbeth* with the class'. Of course, the overwhelming desire to get the play finished in the time frame available is completely understandable; however, she also needed to think about the learning she wanted her students to master rather than simply the action of reading through the act. Did she simply want them to have a basic understanding of the plot in that act? She reflected that it was likely to be much more than this. There are many skills she might want to teach or reinforce – for example, getting them to practise selecting short relevant quotations to support their views, to analyse the language of the quotations in greater depth or to practise using key linguistic terms. The list of possible learning objectives is immense, which is why it is essential to give the intended learning real thought in your planning first, so you can focus students on the key skill or objective rather than just ploughing through the topic content.

We have all taught lessons when we have been much less sharply focused on the learning objectives and have instead concentrated much more on the 'doing' – creating the web page, writing the essay, reviewing the product. However, when this happens the learning can be unfocused and therefore less successful. If the intended learning isn't flagged up to the students before they start, they won't be clear about what they should have learned during the session. In contrast, a well-defined focus helps the learning to stick because the intended learning, skills or knowledge are made transparent and remain the centre of the lesson.

Once you have decided on the key intended learning, it can also be useful to reflect on the following thinking points.

Thinking point

- What might be the tricky aspects to securing this learning?

- What do your past experiences of teaching this topic tell you?

- How might you link this learning or skill to previous work the class have undertaken?

- Do different individuals in the group need additional support or extra challenge? How might this best be achieved?

- Do you need to introduce or remind the class about any key terms or vocabulary? How will you make this memorable?

- How will you know when the pupils are successful? How will you check this?

- How are you intending to help the class reinforce and remember the key learning from this lesson? How can you make it stick?

It is important to get students thinking about what they might already know about this area or topic before you start teaching, rather than just presuming that you know where they are in their learning. Not doing this effectively can really impede progress, as we will see in Chapter 5. Sometimes just starting the lesson by giving the students five minutes to complete a 'brain dump' to list all the information they know about the topic can provide a useful starting point, particularly if you ask them to share one thing they think others in the room might not have thought of. If this seems a bit overwhelming for your group, perhaps ask them to list five things they already know about the topic. Alternatively, show them a piece of work about the topic with some errors in and ask them to see how many they can spot and correct.

However you do it, it is necessary to find a way to correctly gauge their current levels of competence. Questions are ideal for checking on students' prior learning and getting their thought processes going. If they are used to reflecting on the thinking and learning progress explicitly, they will gain a better understanding of what they can do to help themselves become better learners.

Student questions

You might like to plan when you could use these to greatest effect:

- What do I already know about this topic?

- What helped me to recall that?

- Do I understand how this topic fits into the whole scheme of study / examination course?

- What key questions or queries do I already have about this topic? How will I ensure that I address them?

- What are the most important aspects and knowledge about this topic?

- How will I record my notes?

- Which parts of the learning did I find tricky or will I need to reinforce?

- What key or specific vocabulary is there? How will I learn this?

- What will I do after the lesson to help make the key learning stick?

Once you have decided on the key learning you would like to take place, then you can think about the most effective teaching techniques to best achieve this outcome. There are myriad different teaching techniques, so which one(s) would best secure the learning? And what resourcing needs to take place ahead of the lesson? Bear in mind that although getting the right resources is essential, it is unrealistic to make every lesson highly dependent on items that take hours of crafting, cutting or laminating. There simply isn't enough time and it simply isn't desirable. Sometimes your resources might well be a set of textbooks and a packet of sticky notes which, if used creatively, can ensure some deep and sticky learning.

You will also want to cultivate a degree of independence and reflection in your pupils. Providing them with swathes of notes and countless hand-outs doesn't serve to achieve this; in fact, it can be counterproductive. Teachers in one school told me that in trying to support and ensure success with their pupils, they had fallen into the trap of doing far too much for them. The pupils were indifferent about bringing the appropriate equipment to lessons because they knew their teachers would provide it. Likewise, why would they bother making and keeping careful notes when they knew that these would be provided for them by the teacher? The pupils lacked accountability for their own learning and the organisation of their work. Not only was this happening in individual lessons, but across time too, which meant the pupils had got into lazy habits that were hard to break. This also meant that they were not used to taking responsibility for revising and developing their own study skills, so they were underachieving in the actual examinations. When they sat their exams, they didn't complete the answers to the highest level and nor did they review and check their work properly.

Planning our lessons to make sure there is individual pupil accountability in every lesson, every day, is an essential way of resolving this issue. Ultimately, it ensures better learning and therefore greater examination success – even if some pupils kick against it initially. Making pupils work harder than us is desirable for making learning stick, even if it is very unpopular with many pupils at first.

Holding back from doing the legwork for your pupils can help them to make better progress, as illustrated by a friend's recent experience. Teaching *The Great Gatsby* for the first time with her A level group, she spent several weeks over the summer carefully reading the novel and making copious notes and detailed references. She made a tailor-made knowledge organiser detailing on just two sides of A4 the most important quotations, moments, themes and motifs.[1] She explained that the process had really helped her to gain detailed knowledge about the novel. She intended to give the knowledge organiser to her class to help them revise it successfully. She proudly showed this to the class in the first few weeks of term and overheard one student say: 'Great, I can use this rather than having to plough through it myself.' She quickly collected them back in again!

She realised that her urge to ensure her students excelled meant that she was in danger of doing so much for them that it prevented them from analysing and thinking deeply for themselves. Instead, she asked the students to create their own knowledge organiser as part of an ongoing revision activity. They subsequently compared these against their peers' and the teacher's knowledge organisers and discussed the differences. I see this a great deal in schools: staff are so keen for their students to do well that they make it too easy for them. Planning activities that promote deep thought are invaluable for enabling retention and securing understanding.

Avoiding planning pitfalls

When we are planning our lessons, it is essential to think about how we will check that the learning we expect to happen actually happens. Although you might have a carefully thought-out lesson plan, it is vital that you are able to flex it to take account of the pupils' learning within the lesson.

---

1   A knowledge organiser is a document, usually just one or two sides of A4, which condenses all the key knowledge that students need to learn about a topic. They are also used for curriculum planning.

A good friend who is a great maths teacher was expecting Ofsted at her school. She had nothing to be concerned about because day after day she teaches fantastic lessons. She told me that she had planned her introduction to algebra very carefully and was therefore feeling confident. However, during the initial part of the lesson, she realised that some pupils had misconceptions – they hadn't understood some vital steps. Although she realised there were issues with the pupils' understanding, instead of stopping, recapping and ironing out these misunderstandings, as she would do usually, she carried on because she was overly concerned about her lesson plan. She had given a copy of this to the observer and therefore felt she needed to continue with the next stage of the lesson – even though most of the class hadn't understood it – because it was on her plan. She found herself saying to the class, 'I know some of you haven't got this step … but we need to get on to the next part.'

Of course, the result was complete confusion or, in her words, 'Maths carnage!' She did something that she wouldn't have done under normal classroom conditions because she was distracted by being observed. Usually, she would take stock, get feedback from her pupils and use this to alter, adapt and amend her lesson accordingly. While the planning process is important, it is equally as important to adapt our teaching to what our pupils are telling us about their learning as the lesson takes place. We need to ask ourselves whether the intended learning is actually sticking, and, if it isn't, what we can do about it.

The tools in our teaching kit that enable us to make this happen relate to different aspects of Assessment for Learning. This definition from the Assessment Reform Group is still one of the most useful: 'Assessment for Learning is the process of seeking and interpreting evidence for use by learners and their teachers to decide where the learners are in their learning, where they need to go and how best to get there.'[2] These include the

---

2 See Patricia Broadfoot, Richard Daugherty, John Gardner, Wynne Harlen, Mary James and Gordon Stobart, *Assessment for Learning: 10 Principles. Research-Based Principles to Guide Classroom Practice Assessment for Learning* (Assessment Reform Group, 2002), p. 3. Available at: https://www.researchgate.net/publication/271849158_Assessment_for_Learning_10_Principles_ Research-based_principles_to_guide_classroom_practice_Assessment_for_Learning.

use of learning objectives, giving and seeking feedback through effective questioning and encouraging pupils to use peer and self-assessment. All these strategies help them to embed their learning and, in turn, become better learners for themselves. We will explore these strategies further in Chapter 6, 7 and 8.

When we are planning our lessons, it is crucial that we design the learning so the pupils are fully engaged. We engage them first through the intended learning and then through interesting, appropriate and varied teaching techniques. Engaging pupils is crucial because we need to make sure they are sufficiently interested in the intended learning before we can hope that they will start to learn effectively and commit key ideas to memory. We all know that if the learning opportunities in the lesson aren't the most interesting thing on offer, the pupils will take the opportunity to become involved in other less educational, but certainly more appealing activities! Although our planning should focus on the intended learning we hope to secure, it is also important that we use the most engaging and sticky methods to help our pupils master this learning. In the Toolkit (Chapters 10 and 11), there are 50 enticing and interactive activities that can be used to make your teaching sticky.

Reinforcing and reviewing previous learning

Of course, the learning might be happening successfully in the lesson, but is the learning being retained by the students after a period of time? Regular revision and revisiting of key skills is critical to success, so we need to think about how to do this in our planning. Even if we are teaching the next part of a topic, it is important to revisit and review prior learning on a regular basis. A mathematics teacher lamented the fact that while her students could master individual topics and score very good end-of-topic test results, they underperformed in mock and end-of-year examinations. As a result, she feared for their overall GCSE results.

Some of the reasons for this became evident when discussing their test papers with the students, and they were all related to the challenge of making learning stick over time. Sometimes they had appeared to master a topic, but in fact they hadn't. They had simply memorised the steps of the process needed to solve equations in a mechanical fashion, without developing a secure understanding of why they were following the steps. There was an appearance of successful understanding but it was only at a surface level. Sometimes they could remember the key topic knowledge required for a specific test at the end of the series of lessons, but it had not been committed to long-term memory. This meant that it could not be recalled readily when it was required later on, or it could be recalled but the student had forgotten how to apply it successfully under examination conditions. Sometimes they only knew how to tackle a problem because they had been repeatedly practising how to complete it after being immersed in it for the lesson. For example, they could recognise that it was a probability question because they had just completed 15 similar practice questions. However, they struggled when they were given an examination paper with questions on a wide variety of topics dispersed across it. They could not easily identify what type of question it was or what tools were required to complete it, or they could not remember the necessary formula or rule to complete it successfully.

Of course, these issues are not confined to the successful deep learning of mathematics. They pertain to most subject areas. The solution is a combination of developing students' independence, thinking about how to teach the topic so the material is sticky in the first place, and establishing a slightly different approach to planning across a course and a series of lessons. We will consider this in detail in the next chapter.

Chapter 4
Planning for Reviewing Learning

The most successful teachers make effective use of planning to mitigate against deceptive surface learning issues. We have all had the experience of being convinced our students have gained a secure understanding of an area, and then this proves not to be the case. It is only when the class sits a test and you start marking the papers that you realise, to your horror, that the learning was only at a very superficial level indeed.

Most teachers divide up the curriculum into discrete teaching topics or units. This makes sense – it is how examination specifications organise the subject content. It also lends a logic and order to learning for students and teachers alike. It ensures that every area of the course is covered and that learning progresses in a sensible fashion. Easier units are tackled before those that are more complex. Students' skills and expertise are developed and supposedly embedded over time. However, as we have seen, it can lead to some students developing a false level of confidence about some areas. It can also mean that the learning isn't secure. Students soon forget a topic once it has been covered.

This worked when coursework, controlled assessments and short examination modules reigned supreme. Once the students had successfully completed their controlled assessment unit on *Romeo and Juliet* or flood defences, there was no need to keep this knowledge fresh in their mind. The learning was complete and could be erased from their memory. Now, most GCSE and A level students need to recall and understand topics for two years. They also need to transform this knowledge using their skills, whether that is essay writing, completing maths problems at a rapid pace (without a calculator) or explaining a scientific process. It is therefore necessary to flex our approaches to planning to take these challenges into account. This doesn't mean taking a scattergun approach to planning learning, but it does mean utilising planning to best help our students retain their learning. It means that the importance of getting students skilled at revisiting, reviewing and retrieving their previous knowledge is greater than ever before.

Important research on the science of remembering gives weight to this approach. German psychologist Hermann Ebbinghaus researched memory and recall over time. His findings illustrate that even though we might think we have learned something, this information is lost at an exponential rate. The implication is that if students do not reinforce their knowledge, and if they are not reminded regularly of the learning, the retention rate will drop steeply right from the first 24 hours. He challenged himself to memorise different things, including sequences of nonsense words, and noted: 'In no single case did I succeed in an errorless reproduction of the series after 24 hours unless I had read them again once or several times.'[1] The figure that follows illustrates how the learning immediately starts to be forgotten – by the end of day 7 very little of the initial learning has been retained. Unless steps are taken to reinforce learning on a regular basis, not much remains after the period of a month.

---

1   Hermann Ebbinghaus, *Memory: A Contribution to Experimental Psychology*, tr. Henry A. Ruger and Clara Bussenius (New York: Windham Press, 2014 [1913]), p. 61.

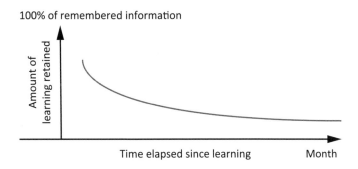

The forgetting curve

Ebbinghaus makes several interesting points relating to the importance of revising and revisiting information. He explained the importance of revisiting material by using the analogy of printing to illustrate how information is instilled into the memory – almost as if it is 'imprinted'. However, he stresses that the number of times something is revisited helps to impress the information much more deeply into the memory:

 As the number of repetitions increases, the series are engraved more and more deeply and indelibly; if the number of repetitions is small, the inscription is but surface deep and only fleeting glimpses of the tracery can be caught; with a somewhat greater number the inscription can, for a time at least, be read at will; as the number of repetitions is still further increased, the deeply cut picture of the series fades out only after ever longer intervals.[2]

The consequences are clear: if we do not revisit and reinforce key learning periodically with our classes, we should not be surprised if learning is lost over a period of time.

The headmaster of Stockport Grammar School, Dr Paul Owen, considers the issue of forgetting in his informative headmaster's blog. He provides

---

2 Ebbinghaus, *Memory*, p. 53.

this helpful comment and illustration on the issue of forgetting and how it can be remedied by effective planning:

 Sometimes teachers test only at the end of a module before moving on to the next. Another approach is to retest some of the previous material at each test ... The same principle may go for revision: start with a few facts and then gradually add in more and more but continue to test everything and not just the new facts. This graphic may help to make the point:[3]

Cumulative units

			4
	2	3	3
1	1	1&2	1&2

Distinct schemes of work

1	2	3	4	5	6

One-off assessments

1	2	3	4	5	6

Frequent quizzes

The advantage of this approach is clear. When previous learning is interleaved with current learning and periodically revisited, the knowledge of the topic is kept fresh in students' minds even while they are being taught new material. Students are required to retrieve their previous learning and make use of it on a regular basis. They are encouraged to check their learning themselves, as the teacher gives them regular mini tests or practice questions. However, these are low-stake tests (not major exams) which means their learning can be practised, checked and reviewed on a regular

---

3   Paul Owen, Memory, *Stockport Grammar School Headmaster's Blog* (25 March 2019). Available at: https://www.stockportgrammar.co.uk/news-and-events/news/memory.

basis. It therefore becomes a good learning habit to adopt. It is important that the periodic testing is low stakes so the students do not feel anxious about it. Instead, they should find it a useful way of checking how well they are retaining knowledge and seeing what gaps still need to be filled.

We can see the issue with retaining learning in the distinct schemes of work approach in the figure on page 49. A long period of time will have passed between scheme 1 and scheme 6, and if opportunities to revisit key learning from previous units aren't made, many students are likely to forget what they once knew. The cumulative units show key aspects of the learning are periodically revisited so that the learning from this area stays fresh in students' minds. It also reminds them that they need to keep this learning active and well-practised – they won't be under the misapprehension that they can 'forget' about previous topics once they have been studied.

Interleaving

This interleaving approach to planning and retesting is useful when you are trying to build and develop students' key skills and reinforce essential subject knowledge in readiness for an examination. As a consultant, I once worked with an English department that was struggling to help some middle-ability pupils with the high level reading skills required for the exam. Although they had spent five or six weeks immersed in teaching these skills, the students' responses still weren't great. They couldn't select appropriate non-fiction quotations readily, they struggled to analyse them in enough depth or detail to show deep understanding and, to top it all, their recall of important knowledge – key literary techniques – was insecure.

In desperation, the teacher started the next half-term by teaching the next unit on *A Christmas Carol,* in accordance with the department schedule. However, because he knew the reading skills from the previous unit had not been well retained, he started each lesson with a brief 10-minute task retrieving and practising the knowledge from this unit. Initially, this was a simple factual recall to build confidence – for example, remembering three specific literary techniques and how to spell them – but as the weeks progressed, these quick tasks demanded greater knowledge and skill from the students. Over time they were making remarkable progress in improving their skills for this paper. The regular short burst of activity, the ability to discuss their answer with a partner and the fact that they received immediate feedback from the teacher (by talking through a good response) meant that they could clearly see how to improve.

Furthermore, when they were told which specific part of the curriculum they were going to be tested on next, the students made an extra effort to revise this area. This was because they knew they would be held accountable for their progress and could take clear steps to make a difference. It also made for good meaningful homework activities because there was a specific focus and a well-defined outcome. The most impressive thing about the whole experience was that the students improved their skills, engagement, confidence and knowledge through a remarkably simple process: a regular 10- or 15-minute retrieval practice. The students were motivated because they could see they were clearly making progress. This meant that when they revised the topic at the end of the year, they already had most of the key learning fresh in their minds and therefore felt successful. They achieved very impressive results on this unit in their final examination – a great outcome all round.

A meaningful recall or retrieval activity from an earlier unit is a good way of keeping previous learning current in the students' minds. Most importantly, the evidence shows that it works! It also reminds them that they will need to be able to successfully access and apply prior learning from the very beginning of the course.

Although I have experimented with different ways of achieving effective retrieval practice, I have found it most successful to conduct this at the start of the lesson. Not only does this avoid the students getting confused with any new learning but it also avoids it taking up too much of the lesson time. Retrieval practice can be an extremely useful settling activity, signalling to the class that the learning is starting by actively revisiting key learning from previous lessons. It becomes part of a regular routine. By working at an efficient pace, the students start to develop the speed and proficiency they need to master for examination success.

Retrieval can take various forms, ranging from the simple but effective (e.g. five quick questions about a previous topic) to much more imaginative approaches. You want the main body of the lesson to focus on the current topic you are teaching, so it makes sense to choose retrieval tasks that can be completed with minimum fuss. It might be desirable to display the questions on the whiteboard so the class can complete them as soon as they arrive and while you are completing the register. This would certainly be a time efficient and purposeful way to start off the lesson. You will also need to ensure that the students receive quick feedback so they can check on their progress, but of course you don't want this activity spilling over and encroaching into the main part of the lesson. This feedback could involve asking class members to suggest likely answers or to run through the correct answers yourself verbally, so that students are able to check their responses. The method doesn't matter as long as they receive feedback on their responses.

Experience suggests that when you first introduce a new approach to a class it can take a while for it to bed in. There will be the inevitable questions and queries, and often a plea to move on with the new lesson material. A good explanation about why it is important to review material and the power of classroom habit over time will soon overcome any objections.

Giving students opportunities to receive immediate feedback about the success of their previous learning is very motivating, as the following example shows. I once had an exceedingly difficult all-boys middle-ability GCSE class. I often started the lesson with a 'quick five' – a fast factual quiz on the learning from the previous lesson. The boys enjoyed recording their scores and charting their progress in the back of their books, noting down anything they got incorrect so they could learn from their mistakes.

It also meant that I was readily able to praise students for their effort and improvement right at the beginning of the lesson. This started things off on a very positive note. It also gave me valuable feedback about the success (or otherwise) of their previous learning. Over time, I set pairs of boys the task of coming up with the quick five for the rest of the class and, of course, the correct answers. They very much enjoyed the challenge of devising some tough questions for their peers. The students were pleasantly competitive and wanted to achieve. Knowing that these quick fives happened on a regular basis was a motivating factor in getting them revising and reviewing their notes in a purposeful fashion. Moreover, because it happened regularly, revision was not an overwhelming task – bite-sized is often best when learning.

The power of habit is extremely helpful for both teacher and learners. Sometimes the lure of just cracking on with the new material can be strong, even when we know how important it is to revisit and embed previous learning. Keeping to a learning routine is easier when it has a catchy name that sets out your expectations – your students will remind you of it too when you are tempted to skip it!

Fix It Fridays

A teacher in one sixth-form college had a successful approach to getting his A level students to review and revisit their previous learning called 'Fix It Fridays'. He would start the lesson by showing them a short piece of work from several units past. It could be anything that needed to be improved or that contained errors, such as a graph, a problem with mistakes in it or a few paragraphs from an essay. The students would then spend 10 minutes individually reworking and improving it to the best standard possible. Then they would work with a partner to check and recheck their response. This gave them another opportunity to improve the work and make appropriate corrections. Finally, the teacher would ask one pair to display their improvements under the visualiser. (A visualiser is a really good tool for sharing work immediately with the whole class: a small lamp-like camera with a flexible head allows examples of students' work, artefacts or pictures to be displayed on the whiteboard so that everyone can view them.) It is also a good motivator and increases accountability because the students know they may be asked to show their work to the whole class. Unlike merely reading aloud or giving a verbal answer, the students can evidence improvements visually. This provides a good opportunity for the class to assess whether it is an effective fix and discuss any misconceptions that might have arisen.

By calling this activity Fix It Fridays – and, of course, completing it on a Friday – it meant that the students readily accepted this as a useful learning routine. It also reminded the teacher that there was real merit in looking back at previous topics and getting his students to review and correct work, even when there was still a good deal of new subject material yet to cover.

Retrieval practice evidence

There is a great deal of research from across the world which shows the benefits of retrieval practice spaced out over the course of study. For example, Pooja K. Agarwal and colleagues found that: 'Over the course of a 5-year applied research project with more than 1,400 middle school students, evidence from a number of studies revealed that retrieval practice in authentic classroom settings improves long-term learning.' Quizzes were found to be particularly effective in enhancing long-term learning. There was also evidence that 'delayed quizzing' (going back to previously taught material) was 'particularly potent for retention. Quizzes with feedback also improved students' learning and metacognitive awareness.'[4]

---

4   Pooja K. Agarwal, Patrice M. Bain and Roger W. Chamberlain, The Value of Applied Research: Retrieval Practice Improves Classroom Learning and Recommendations from a Teacher, a Principal, and a Scientist. *Educational Psychology Review*, 24(3) (2012): 437–448. Abstract available at: https://link.springer.com/article/10.1007/s10648-012-9210-2.

Regardless of the research evidence, the most important thing is to think about the pupils you teach. How can you best have success in your classroom so that pupils' learning and achievement are improving over time? Getting them to actively remember and recall their previous learning is helpful, but, of course, you also need to think about their learning needs and how best to motivate them to take part in revisiting activities. Ensuring that our pupils understand why we are asking them to do something is particularly significant. If we can encourage them to develop their metacognitive skills and think about the learning they are doing, and to what extent it is effective, they will be much more motivated and this, in turn, will help to maximise their progress still further.

Retrieval activities that work

Although a simple quiz can be highly effective, there are some successful retrieval activities that work well for a range of different subjects. For example, posing three questions or asking pupils to prepare five questions to ask each other ahead of the lesson can be both time efficient and effective in embedding learning. However, it is a good idea to mix up your approach by using different retrieval activities. This will keep it interesting for your pupils and will help to prevent them becoming complacent about their learning. Many of the sticky learning activities in the Toolkit (Chapters 10 and 11) can also be easily adapted or used in their current form as retrieval activities.

1. Blockbusters

Students will be too young to remember the classic teatime TV programme *Blockbusters*, but the concept can be used to create a pacy retrieval activity. Display some connecting hexagons on the whiteboard. Each hexagon must have a piece of important information in it – for example, for students studying practices in Judaism (GCSE RE) you might display Havdalah, Shabbat, Mitzvot, Rosh Hashanah, Shul and Torah.

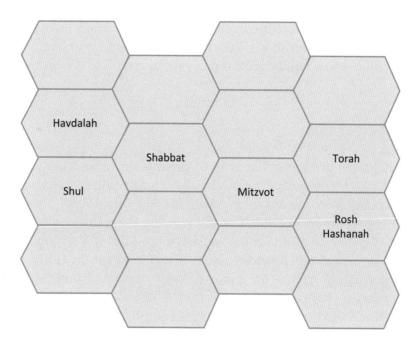

In pairs, the students must come up with a question where the answer is the word in the hexagon. They should take it in turns to ask questions until they make it across the board. The best questions can then be shared with the class. This activity can be adapted by using images instead. This can increase the level of challenge since they also must identify what is shown in the pictures.

2. Thought tumble

Ask the students to consider a specific area they have studied previously – for example, Mr Birling's presentation in Act 1 of *An Inspector Calls* (GCSE English), Milgram's agency theory (GCSE / A level psychology) or information about SLR cameras (GCSE photography). Give them five minutes to note down as many things as they can remember about the topic. They should underline three that they think other students might have forgotten. They can then share these with the class. It is a quick but useful way of getting students to recall key information – the time pressure replicates the fast thinking that will be required in examinations.

3. Spider diagrams

Spider diagrams are a familiar way of organising connecting ideas and concepts linked to a central topic visually. To test pupils' retrieval skills show them half a completed spider diagram. They then have five minutes to fill in and complete as much of the missing diagram as possible. For example, a spider diagram on the causes of the French Revolution might include a branch about financial issues under which you could include certain information, such as the names of the finance ministers, but miss off some key dates. There might be strands called Estates-General or Enlightenment ideas, but you could leave them incomplete. This task encourages deep thinking and really tests pupils' detailed knowledge of the subject. It is also very useful for examination practice since it helps them plan the content of their essays quickly and confidently.

4. Loop cards

Hand out cards on one side of which there is a question and on the other side the answer to a different question. Ask the students to stand up (this keeps them alert!). One student starts by reading out their question – for example, 'What is the chemical symbol for lead?' The rest of the class study their answers and the student with the correct answer on their card calls it out 'Pb'. This student then turns over their card and asks their question: 'Name one of the chemical properties of lead.' And so on. The students should sit down when they have answered.

The idea is that all the students should be focused on listening out for the answer. This is best arranged by asking the students to stand up; they sit down when they have answered correctly. This is a good activity for revising key information because all the students are focused on looking out for the correct answer, so they are all listening and thinking intently. It is a favoured teaching technique with science teachers, but it works effectively for any topic when there are short specific answers to knowledge-based questions. Even if the class completes the task, you can retest them on the same questions later on, mixing up the cards and challenging them to complete it more quickly, thereby demonstrating their competency with the material.

5. Pick from the past

Periodically, ask the pupils to devise several questions about the topic they are studying. Collect these in and store them in an A4 envelope. At the start of a lesson, a pupil selects four or five of these questions at random and poses them to the class. Individuals should note down their responses and the correct answer is then discussed. The benefit of this approach is that the pupils have to retrieve information from across the period of study rather than from just the current session.

Thinking point

- How do you arrange the curriculum so that students can revisit prior learning? Are there any adaptations you could make to your approach?

- What use do you make of different retrieval activities to get the students accessing and using previous knowledge?

- How effectively can the students identify the requirements of a specific examination question when seen out of context?

- How might you encourage the students to feel motivated and engaged by completing retrieval practice?

- Can you get your students engaged in creating mini tests or questions to quiz each other?

- How do you encourage the students to chart their own progress?

- How far do you encourage the students to learn from their mistakes?

- How will you use the information generated from retrieval practice to help inform your future teaching?

Chapter 5
A Sticky Lesson in Action

 Tell me and I forget. Teach me and I remember. Involve me and I learn.

Anon.

There are countless ways to teach a great lesson in which the learning is made sticky and retained by students. However, it is worthwhile looking at an actual example of a lesson to see how one teacher sets out to make learning memorable for her students.

The notes on the lesson that follows were made by a class teacher who was observing her class being taught a GCSE revision lesson by a consultant.[1] The class teacher made some notes about what was effective about the teaching and learning she observed. When you read the write-up of the lesson, consider: what does the teacher do to make this an effective and engaging learning experience for the students? How does she try to ensure that the learning is memorable? What is the observer surprised by? The students are in a middle-ability class just a few months away from their final GCSE examinations, so the focus of the lesson is revision of a previously taught topic.

---

1   I would like to thank Charlotte Cross, assistant head of teaching and learning at Fairfax Multi-Academy Trust, for granting me permission to use her notes in this chapter.

Summary of positive observations

The students were very engaged and worked well, even though they didn't know the teacher. She used specific praise very effectively and engaged them, valuing their contributions. This encouraged them to want to offer their ideas and get involved in the lesson.

Assessment for Learning

The lesson started with an assessment of what the students knew: she asked them for five things found in persuasive writing. I thought they would know this (it has been covered a lot) but they didn't. This reminded me not to make assumptions about knowledge – that just because I have taught something doesn't mean they have learned it.

Teaching

Questioning was extremely effective – she never accepted the first answer and probed more and more all the time. This deepened the students' thinking and made them give fuller responses. All the teaching and activities were linked explicitly to the exam criteria. The pace of the lesson was purposeful. The students were asked to provide feedback, annotate or write, which kept them on their toes throughout the lesson. She continually worked the classroom – standing at the front when talking, and moving around individual students and giving one-to-one motivation as and when needed.

Learning

She showed them three exemplars, which they had to rank and say why they got the grades they did. There was a high level of challenge here as even though they were 4/5 borderline students she showed them a grade 7 response. This demonstrated high expectations and built confidence as there were elements of a grade 7 answer they could accomplish.

The students then completed part of a GCSE exam paper and marked each other's responses using clear success criteria. The six criteria were also replicated on a writing wheel which summarised the different aspects of successful writing – for example, using effective vocabulary and a range of sentence structures. They then looked at how to improve their work by scoring each aspect of their writing using the criteria. What was good about this was that it was simple but also graded. It wasn't a matter of 'Have you done this or not?'; rather it encouraged evaluation by asking how effectively they had addressed each skill. The hardest task for the students was writing their own response using precisely 45 words as well as effective punctuation, literary devices and interesting adjectives. She then read out work from a range of students to share effective practice. The students were obviously challenged throughout the lesson, and it was particularly demanding at the end when the teacher and the students self-assessed what they could do better as a result of the lesson.

Environment

Praise was a major factor throughout the lesson. The students were given clear feedback about their contribution. There was a good use of humour to get them onside and to make herself non-threatening. She was also very respectful/formal, referring to the students as 'sir' and 'miss' rather than by name – a useful tactic if names are not known. Behaviour was good as the students were engaged. There weren't hundreds of resources but there were a range of activities and everything was focused on the exam.

Sticky notes were given to all of the students to ensure they had each contributed and were engaged. They were asked to write their name on the note at the start of the lesson and the teacher collected them back in when they had answered a question. This helped her to keep track of who had and hadn't contributed to the session. All the students made rapid and sustained progress.

Thinking point

- What seemed to you the most successful aspect of the lesson?

- Are there any teaching techniques that you find interesting?

- Have you ever observed your class being taught a revision session by another teacher?

- Do you think there might be any benefits to arranging this? What area or topic would you be most interested in seeing revised?

Observations on the lesson

There are hundreds of different ways that the teacher could have revised this topic effectively with the class, but it was successful for several key reasons.

Planning

The teacher starts by checking the pupils' prior knowledge before the lesson gets underway. This is of critical importance because the findings from this might have altered the whole course of the lesson. This initial activity allowed the teacher to gauge the understanding of the class, rather than just presuming what they already knew. She could have done this in various ways, but simply asking them to name five things about the topic is a quick way to get an accurate snapshot of what the pupils already know. It is interesting that the class teacher believed they would already know the key aspects of persuasive writing, because she had taught it to them before, but she was mistaken. This demonstrates the importance of not taking our pupils' prior learning for granted. It shows why it is necessary to revise and to get them to regularly go back over their learning in order for them to deeply embed it.

The rest of the lesson is divided up into several different purposeful sections, which means the pupils could see that their learning was progressing in a clear and organised way. Of course, the teacher might have adjusted or completely changed her activities as the lesson developed, depending on the feedback she received. She includes a range of varied learning activities, all of which demand involvement and active participation by all the pupils – they couldn't opt out of the learning experience. This is crucial not only for ensuring that learning sticks, but also that it is appropriately challenging for all.

Thinking point

- What opportunities do you take to check pupils' prior learning and knowledge at the start of a session?

- How can you be sure that you get an accurate reading from all pupils?

- How do you plan activities to maximise the involvement of all pupils? How do you ensure that there are no passengers in any of your lessons?

- How can you ensure that the learning activities in the lesson are pitched at the right level for the pupils' ability?

- How do you plan so that you take account of the forgetting curve when revising with your class?

Engagement

The lesson is engaging because it has an appropriate pace that helps to develop the pupils' learning in a purposeful way. Pace doesn't refer to the speed of teaching (although it is often mistaken as such); it relates to the rate of the pupils' learning. The effective teacher decides when the next learning episode needs to start or whether the pupils are still deeply absorbed in what they are currently learning and so it can continue for a while longer. The pupils aren't left on tasks for so long that they lose interest or motivation. There are clear, definable success criteria: they are motivated to complete the task because they know what is expected from them. They are asked for well-defined answers (such as finding five things) to complete a short piece of work of a specific given length or to undertake a paired activity that has a definite outcome and success criteria. Clarity is important in ensuring that pupils are committed to a task.

Challenge

The teacher provides a suitable resource to showcase what pupils could be aiming for, which helps to raise expectations about the outcomes of their work. Interestingly, the sample work is set several grades higher than the pupils' current level. This inspires learning ambition by showing them that although they are not currently achieving at this level, they can still benefit from seeing exemplary work. They are encouraged to find inspiration and practical takeaways by exploring the inspirational higher level work. It is crucial to raise the bar for all pupils, so tasks should be suitably challenging and push all learners on to the next stage of their learning. There is a compendium of engaging lesson activities in the Toolkit which can be used to engage and challenge your pupils. The teacher's questioning, which constantly probes and pushes the pupils further, is also a key part of the challenge (there is more on this in Chapters 7 and 8).

Reviewing learning and target-setting

The pupils are frequently encouraged to reflect on their learning. Although the teacher's initial question is significant in gauging the pupils' level of knowledge at the start of the lesson, it also signposts to them where they are currently with their learning. As the observer notes, the pupils don't have a secure basis of knowledge to start with. This early snapshot demonstrates to the pupils just how much progress they have made by the end of the lesson. This is one of the most helpful strategies for encouraging pupil motivation. The level of reflection required by the pupils is more advanced by the end of the lesson because they are now thinking about their own progress and next steps in an evaluative way by using the self-assessment writing wheel. This approach develops their reflective skills rather than simply requiring them to measure their progress.

Target-setting is best done periodically, otherwise pupils are forever setting targets in each lesson rather than accomplishing meaningful improvements across a short series of lessons. Well-defined success criteria means that the pupils have a clear idea about what they are working towards and this can help to make the task seem achievable. Of course, these skills need to be embedded over time before they can be assumed to be secure.

Thinking point

- What was it about the teaching in the lesson that meant the pupils were likely to have secured the intended learning?

- Which lesson ideas and activities have you used recently that have been particularly successful in inspiring pupils?

- Think about a lesson that was less effective in engaging pupils. Why do you think this was the case? Are there any tweaks you could make to improve the activity or task? Or do they need to be completely changed or reworked?

- How do you gauge when it is the right time to change or develop a task to ensure that pupils remain engaged? How do you make sure they have derived the maximum learning benefit from the activity?

- What helps you to determine the correct degree of challenge so that all pupils are motivated in lessons and that the tasks have the correct level of desirable difficulty?

- Does giving pupils precise guidelines, clear success criteria and specific word limits help to focus and encourage them? Is this something you do? What might be the learning benefits of doing this? Are there any drawbacks to this approach?

Chapter 6
Questioning for Learning and Feedback

 Who questions much, shall learn much, and retain much.

Francis Bacon (attrib.)

Questioning is the power tool of teaching. There are many practices that improve pupil progress, but great questioning is vital in helping learning to stick. Most importantly, it happens in every single learning experience. It is one of the few areas of teaching that is experienced *every* day by *all* pupils, and if managed well it has a huge impact on making learning memorable: 'Good questions lead to improved comprehension, learning, and memory among school children.'[1]

Think for a moment about questioning in the classroom: what do you hear? Who do you typically imagine is asking the questions? Questioning has been the subject of much research. How many questions do you think you have asked as a teacher? Would it surprise you to learn that if you have been teaching for between five and ten years then you have probably asked from 'a quarter to a half a million questions'.[2] If you have not been teaching that long then the number of questions is still impressive: 'Even a student

1 Scotty D. Craig, Jeremiah Sullins, Amy Witherspoon and Barry Gholson, The Deep-Level-Reasoning-Question Effect: The Role of Dialogue and Deep-Level-Reasoning Questions During Vicarious Learning, *Cognition and Instruction*, 24(4) (2006): 565–591 at 567.
2 Edward C. Wragg and George Brown, *Questioning in the Secondary School* (London and New York: RoutledgeFalmer, 2001), p. 15.

teacher spending, say, ten weeks in a school teaching half a timetable may well ask five to ten thousand questions.'[3] After all, Kathleen Cotton found that 'questioning was the second most dominant teaching method after teacher talk ... with teachers spending between 35–50% of teaching time posing questions'.[4] It really needs to count. Perhaps we should be asking, how effective are these questions? How can questioning best be managed to make learning memorable and successful?

There is a huge amount to be said regarding questioning, but we are going to focus on those aspects that really help learning to stick. There are references in the bibliography at the back of the book that offer detail on where you can find further reading related to this important area.

Who asks questions?

Most questions in lessons are posed by the teacher to the pupils. This is only to be expected since it is the teacher who has the subject expertise and they want to pass this on. Questioning checks to what extent this has been successful. However, the evidence tells us that getting pupils involved in asking questions to the teacher and to one another reaps huge learning rewards. There are several reasons for this. When a pupil poses a question they have had to think about the topic – and there are ways of making them think hard! Asking a question also gives them the opportunity to clarify their ideas and push their understanding further. Most importantly, it gives them the chance to remedy any misconceptions in their comprehension. This is crucial because often the reason that learning doesn't stick is because the main principles of an area have not been properly understood. Even worse, the key knowledge might have been learned incorrectly. For

---

3 Wragg and Brown, *Questioning in the Secondary School*, p. 15.
4 Kathleen Cotton, Classroom Questioning. School Improvement Research Series, Close-Up #5 (1988). Available at: https://educationnorthwest.org/resources/classroom-questioning, quoted in Hattie *Visible Learning*, p. 182.

pupils' learning to progress, they need a very firm foundation of under-standing because more complex aspects build on this basic knowledge.

False positives

Of course, when a pupil answers a teacher's question correctly, it doesn't always mean they have fully understood the concept. They might just be guessing, parroting an answer or giving an answer that they think the teacher wants to hear. As Wragg observes, 'their understanding may be imperfect, even if an answer is correct'.[5] This is a real problem because it clouds our ability to judge how successfully learning has been understood. This can happen if we use too many closed questions, which are often used to check factual understanding and recall. Closed questions don't probe a pupil's understanding in the same way that an open question does, however – so they often don't alert us exactly to the stumbling blocks to understanding. The yes, no or one-word answer doesn't give us sufficient information to be sure that learning has really been mastered or whether it was just a lucky guess.

There are clear reasons for encouraging more questions by pupils. How-ever, I would challenge you to observe a range of different lessons because the opportunities for pupils to ask good learning questions are often far fewer than you might expect. Look out for moments when the pupils' learning could be significantly deepened by being actively encouraged to ask more questions.

---

5 Wragg and Brown, *Questioning in the Secondary School*, p. 43.

Breaking down the barriers

What are the barriers to pupils asking learning questions? By 'learning questions' I mean questions that further the learning in the lesson, rather than questions about anything else. (Obviously, pupils ask questions, but these are often requests for equipment loans, toilet breaks and so on.) The three main barriers to pupils posing actual learning questions are best summarised as: lack of planned opportunities, a restrictive lesson climate, and that it is not seen as adding to the learning.

Time issues

The eternal refrain of the busy teacher is 'there isn't enough time'. When we are time pressed, we often think we don't have the luxury of allowing pupil questions. However, making time for this can give us a valuable insight into how successfully they are learning, or not. It is an opportunity to address any issues early on before misconceptions become embedded, so it is the ultimate time-saver! Although we might believe that our pupils will readily ask questions if they need to, it can feel very daunting to ask an unscheduled question in front of the whole class. Unless questioning opportunities are expected and encouraged, then in many classrooms they simply won't happen. A colleague schedules specific time for questioning into her lesson plan – she makes sure it happens because the rewards are so great.

Classroom climate issues

We considered classroom climate in Chapter 2, but it is so important in making questioning successful that it deserves to be briefly mentioned with this focus. Much will be gained if we can create an atmosphere in our lessons which encourages and values pupils' responses. Do our pupils feel confident enough to ask questions that admit their confusion, that seek clarification or that explore an issue by pushing their learning further through searching questions? The teacher who fears an unexpected question will not create a successful learning atmosphere. We are all concerned about the prospect of losing control of a lesson through too many pupil responses. However, there are various strategies that can be employed to prevent this, including giving individual pupils sticky notes or cards with their name on so that when they ask a question or contribute these can be collected in. It is a brilliant way of keeping track of who is contributing and who is trying to remain under the radar, so these pupils can be called on to participate. Focusing on those individuals who have not participated can help to deter those pupils who might normally try to monopolise the session from taking over. Some primary colleagues take this further by also issuing pupils with 'talk tokens', in the form of a limited number of counters that they can 'spend' when they wish to answer a question. As each pupil receives a limited number of these, they are forced to think carefully about when they want to use them.

Why pupils asking questions helps learning

As an adviser, I undertake a great many lesson observations. These highlight how teachers can make learning memorable but also some of the obstacles. In one science lesson, the pupils were learning successfully and this was due in large part to the questioning involved. The pupils were encouraged to pose questions. These really helped to cement understanding, not just for the pupil asking the question but for others in the class too. After all, it is unlikely that only one pupil will have that query, even if they lack the confidence to express it. The pupils raised questions for a variety of reasons: there was the inevitable task clarification question ('Do we need to draw the diagram?') as well as several thoughtful questions. These showed that the pupils were really thinking about the topic and grappling with their newly acquired knowledge. So, what was it about the lesson that was so successful?

Firstly, the teacher gave a lively and detailed description of the carbon cycle using a useful visual aid. They asked a range of questions to check the pupils' understanding. Next, to help cement this learning, the pupils were asked to complete a task on the carbon cycle and to record it as a diagram. Before the pupils started on the independent task, the teacher asked: 'What questions do you still have about the carbon cycle?' In many lessons teachers ask, 'Do you have any questions?' and there is often complete silence. This doesn't mean that there aren't any questions or that there is complete understanding. When I am observing lessons from the back of the room, pupils often turn to me once a task is underway and ask me the questions they would have liked to have asked their teacher. This might be clarification of the task ('What do we have to do?'), a fundamental question related to basic understanding of the topic they have missed ('What is a prime number?'), a question that shows their misconceptions ('Why isn't 1 a prime number?') or a deeper question about the subject '(Why are prime numbers important in maths?').

The slight change of emphasis in the science teacher's question yields much richer responses and, crucially, lightens the classroom tone. It demonstrates that it is expected that pupils will have queries. 'What questions do you have?' invites speculation from the pupils and encourages them to give you feedback about aspects they are still grappling with. Of course, just posing this question won't ensure that pupils are willing to divulge the gaps in their knowledge.

The lesson climate is set by our responses to the questions the pupils pose. We give information both through what we say and through our non-verbal communication. Sometimes pupils come up with unusual enquiries and you wonder, where on earth did they get such an idea? Sometimes their questions will inspire and humble you because you have not thought of the topic in that way before. Sometimes they have misunderstood things so badly that you can't believe it – you thought you had made it clear! However, if we respond to pupils tactlessly or sarcastically this can be absolutely crushing for the pupil. We can't show our exasperation (however much we might feel it at that moment). We need to withhold judgement and show encouragement instead. We must reflect and amend our explanations so they do understand.

Pupils' questions reveal both their thought processes and the gaps in their understanding. So, some of the questions posed by the pupils in the science lesson were predictable, but others less so:

1. What does photosynthesis mean?

2. Is it only cows that produce carbon?

3. Why is it called a cycle?

4. Is it like the water cycle?

5. What are microorganisms?

6. Why do the arrows only go one way?

7. How important is the carbon cycle?

These questions give the teacher opportunities to correct misunderstandings. Several show that the scientific language used about the cycle is insecure. The teacher took a great learning opportunity by discussing what the prefix 'photo' meant and how it could be remembered. Some of the other questions (such as 4 and 6) provide opportunities for the pupils to make links with other parts of their science studies. Question 7 is an interesting one – a potentially high level question which encourages evaluation. Before responding, the teacher decided to ask the class to discuss their ideas about it in pairs to get them to think more deeply about it. This is a simple but highly effective teaching technique that involved all the pupils.

The pupils were making really good progress in science – their books and assessments showed this. The teacher told me that he had a mantra which changed the pupils' approach and encouraged their involvement: 'I tell my class that there is no such thing as a stupid question.' It's simple, but it works. Learning was also embedded because he encouraged other pupils to answer and explain questions for their peers. Not only did this help to secure their own learning, but it also helped him to see whether it was a common misconception across the class or an individual query.

John Hattie, master reviewer of research, gives us the critical reminder: 'Perhaps more important than teacher questioning is analysing the questions that students ask.'[6] It is these questions that help us to make learning sticky for pupils, as we realise what their perceptions are. They help us to assess the depth of their knowledge and thereby remove the barriers to their understanding.

There are various engaging strategies in the Toolkit to help pupils devise questions for themselves and their peers which will develop their metacognitive muscles. Activities such as the delicious 'Doughnut Reading Round' or 'Traffic Lights Quiz' will really enliven lessons, get everybody involved and encourage deep thinking by the pupils. There is also the reference to various question stems initially devised by Bloom (and subsequently revised by Lorin Anderson and David Krathwol[7]) which can be used by pupils to help them formulate better quality questions to ask. In the next chapter we will consider why making mistakes is so beneficial and further develop the contribution of questioning to this area.

---

6 Hattie, *Visible Learning*, p. 183.
7 Lorin W. Anderson and David R. Krathwohl, *A Taxonomy for Learning, Teaching and Assessing: A Revision of Bloom's Taxonomy of Educational Objectives* (New York: Longman, 2001).

Thinking point

- How do you try to establish a supportive classroom environment that will encourage participation by all?

- Are you aware of your non-verbal communication when you ask questions and receive answers from pupils?

- How do you encourage pupils who seek clarification by asking questions in class?

- What teaching activities do you undertake to ensure that foundation knowledge is deeply secured by your pupils?

- How do you make time for questioning in your lessons?

- What do you do to help your pupils to ask good learning questions?

- How do you make use of pupils' questions to influence your teaching?

- How do you get pupils involved in answering their peers' questions?

Chapter 7
The Importance of Engaging with Getting Things Wrong

 If we embrace and even study errors in our classrooms, students may actually learn more.

Amy Eva

There is subject knowledge that all pupils need to secure. You want them to know these essentials inside out so they can draw on them automatically. Likewise, you want them to be able to utilise certain skills easily and instinctively, whether that is writing in paragraphs, drawing a line graph or making good pastry. Much of this knowledge is inevitably topic specific, such as knowing the relevant vocabulary to describe different hobbies in French, remembering key quotations from Ibsen or understanding the rules of rugby. However, in any subject there will be key knowledge that underpins understanding and performance across the subject as a whole – for example, having a secure command of the identification, role, use and spelling of literary terms in English literature. This core information is needed from primary school through to university level studies – at varying levels of complexity, of course.

It is important that these building blocks of knowledge are deeply embedded as they provide the foundation for more advanced learning. However, many teachers often feel frustrated that the skills and knowledge taught to pupils in the earlier years are still patchy at Year 11: there are surprising issues with retention. Pupils still have gaps in their understanding and are still making mistakes – sometimes quite basic ones.

One of the reasons for these gaps is a persistent lack of pupil participation in lessons. Researcher John Hattie calls these pupils 'physically present, but psychologically absent'.[1] Pupils don't expose their lack of knowledge to either their teacher or themselves because they don't actively engage in the lesson. However, pupils need to see the importance of engaging with the lesson activity in order to recognise how getting things wrong can actually help them to become better learners. Embedded learning happens when pupils practise recalling and applying what they have learned previously. But it is true that in some classrooms some of them can get away with opting out of this process and become silent passengers.

We might think that this doesn't happen in our lessons, but the evidence shows that teachers believe that many more pupils have been involved in questioning sessions than is actually the case. I saw an example of this when I led a whole-school INSET. The deputy head had previously surveyed both pupils and staff about a range of teaching approaches. She displayed various results on the screen: staff were confident that well over 95% of pupils answered questions regularly in their lessons. However, when the pupils were asked whether they regularly answered questions this fell by more than 30%! The staff were astounded. Perhaps they had become too caught up in the immediacy of the lesson activities to be able to easily keep track of who had contributed?

The main reason that pupils give for not wanting to join in is the fear of getting things wrong. Whatever the issue, these passive passengers need to be engaged so that their responses can be heard and acted upon. The gap between our perception of what happens in lessons and what really happens is important. It explains dips in performance of those pupils who are coasting in lessons and whose lack of progress has been hidden.

Many of the strategies in the Toolkit will help to embed pupils' understanding because they allow for the teacher to pose questions or activities that demand the participation of everyone. Most pupils need to undertake activities that really give them time to mull over the learning, record it,

---

1 Hattie, *Visible Learning*, p. 250.

discuss it and try things out, which is where the Toolkit activities really come into their own.

Many techniques give pupils purposeful time to think about their responses. This is important: a large amount of research indicates that the average thinking time after a teacher poses a question is less than a second.[2] If you don't believe me, observe a few lessons or even catch yourself after you have asked a question! Unsurprisingly, this means that pupils' answers lack the appropriate depth and are not fully thought-through. Even if we are running a quick questioning session to briefly recap knowledge, counting in our heads to three before inviting pupil responses will improve the quality of their responses because they will have enough time to think. It will also make for a more accurate reading of the pupils' overall competency in this area.

Importantly, it is not the case that pupils either know something or they don't. It's not that simple. There are degrees of understanding and competency. Sometimes they need to grapple with the task. Sometimes they need to pause and check so they don't make a silly mistake. Sometimes they need to think hard about the subtleties of the topic and retrieve the information required to answer the question or complete the task. The answer might be on the tip of their tongue. It isn't as simple as either knowing something or not – there are degrees. There have also been numerous studies on the significance of reviewing and forgetting previous learning in securing long-term knowledge in the memory. For example, Bjork observes that 'forgetting often enhances subsequent learning'.[3] This explains why it is more effective to revise a topic in 20-minute chunks over a period of time rather than study a single topic all day. Better learning and long-term retention occurs by revisiting a topic, rather than an immersive activity, because 'retrieval is a powerful memory modifier'.[4] There are clear implications

---

2   Mary Budd Rowe, *Teaching Science as Continuous Inquiry: A Basic* (New York: McGraw Hill, 1978).

3   Bjork and Bjork, Making Things Hard on Yourself, p. 61.

4   Bjork and Bjork, Making Things Hard on Yourself, p. 61.

here for the effectiveness of whole study days on a single subject and the ideal length of our revision sessions.

Why incorrect answers help us

Incorrect answers can help us, but only if we deal with them in the right way. We can feel dismayed when students give us an incorrect answer, so we sometimes ask the students who we know will give us the correct response. We feel a sense of relief and their accurate response means we can progress on to the next stage of the lesson. But the right answers from reliable students deceive us into thinking that everyone has understood. (Moreover, if all the students are getting everything right all the time, it must surely indicate that the lessons lack challenge. They are ready for more demanding learning that will accelerate their progress.) An incorrect answer gives us a good opportunity to explore the reasoning behind it and think about how we can make the learning stickier for all students. There are ways of doing this that are more successful than others, as the following example demonstrates.

I was once invited to teach some very able GCSE students as a guest teacher in a school in Wales in preparation for their examinations. It was lesson 6 at the end of an exhausting day. They were the top set, so I started the session by posing a challenging question. One boy immediately offered an answer – an incorrect one based on a typical mistake caused by not thinking things through carefully. My disappointment must have shown on my face when I corrected his response. I noticed that he then made no further contribution during the rest of the session. I realised that I had managed this interaction poorly on several levels. Not only had the student's belief in himself as a successful learner been damaged, but not all the class were actively involved in the thinking process. I was not convinced they had really learned from my correction. It wasn't my best lesson!

One of the joys of teaching is having the opportunity to improve on your practice. Within a fortnight, I taught the same lesson to a different class and a similar mistake occurred: an answer given too quickly that hadn't been fully thought-through. On this occasion, I paused, repeated the student's response and asked everyone to reflect on it in pairs. Did they agree or disagree? What was their reasoning? Some animated discussion took place for a few minutes. The student who had originally given the wrong answer responded, 'I realise I was wrong. The answer is … because of …' He was thrilled to correct himself and his self-esteem was clearly intact. After congratulating him on his improved thinking, we spent a few minutes as a class reflecting on the question and why it was so often answered incorrectly. This time the student felt so much better about himself and, importantly, his classmates also had the opportunity to learn from the common error by reflecting for themselves. Much better learning and thinking all round! It is these small tweaks in our teaching approach that really improve learning.

Getting students to reflect on their answers and asking them to actually think about the quality of their responses is essential. As a well-meaning teacher, it is easy to jump in too quickly to close the gap and correct their responses. Of course, it is vital that the correct answer is understood, but all too often we do it without allowing students to strive and think for themselves. It is this striving and grappling with a response that leads to deeper understanding and prepares them for being able to work independently. When students feel they have the self-efficacy to improve their learning outcomes, they will be willing to try more challenging tasks. Self-efficacy is an individual's judgement about 'how well one can execute courses of action required to deal with prospective situations'.[5] In order for this to happen, we must not be afraid of incorrect answers; they are necessary for the development of good learning. Self-efficacy means students can persevere with challenging tasks and become successful learners. It is this belief in their own ability to improve, think for themselves and tackle tricky tasks

---

5   Albert Bandura quoted in Michael P. Carey and Andrew D. Forsyth, Teaching Tip Sheet: Self-Efficacy, *American Psychological Association* (2009). Available at: https://www.apa.org/pi/aids/resources/education/self-efficacy.

that leads to great learning gains. However, we need to provide opportunities for this to develop.

Here are some useful phrases to use to promote self-efficacy around tricky learning with your students:

- Why do you think many students often get this question wrong?

- What assumptions do students sometimes make about this topic?

- How can we remember the steps/process/term for next time?

- What other topics did you find tricky? What helped you master them?

- Is that always the case?

- Can you think of another example where this happens?

- What was tricky about this question/task? What helped you complete it?

- What do you think is the most important thing you have learned from this?

- How might you tackle this differently next time?

- If you get stuck on this in the examination, what will you do first?

- What are you most pleased about with your learning today?

Multiple-choice questions: do they help learning stick?

Historically, multiple-choice questions have had a bad press. We might remember them from our own school days: they never felt like a satisfactory test of our understanding, particularly when some of the alternative answers were so extreme that they made the correct choice all too easy to pick out. It was also possible to gain a decent mark by guessing C for all those questions you didn't know! Things have since changed, however. Research by Arnold Glass and Neha Sinha has shown that a careful use of well thought-out multiple-choice questions can make a significant contribution to helping the right learning stick: 'Distributed multiple-choice questioning has been demonstrated to be an effective and efficient instructional method for improving examination performance for a variety of student populations and topics.'[6]

Importantly, multiple-choice questions make it easy to involve all students, whether by asking them to hold up a mini whiteboard displaying their answer or using commercial clickers or interactive games such as Kahoot! or Plickers to select the correct response. Having the opportunity to see each individual's answer is critical as it reveals misconceptions in specific areas. As Caroline Wylie and Dylan Wiliam observe: 'given the constrained choices of a multiple-choice question, students' answers will cluster into a small number of categories, thus further assisting teachers process and interpret the information'.[7] Gaining accurate feedback about students' current level of understanding in real time in a lesson (rather than when marking their work later on) is an essential part of improving learning. It

---

6 Arnold L. Glass and Neha Sinha, Multiple Choice Questioning is an Efficient Instructional Methodology That May Be Widely Implemented in Academic Courses to Improve Exam Performance, *Current Directions in Psychological Science*, 22(6) (2013): 471–477 at 475.

7 Caroline Wylie and Dylan Wiliam, Diagnostic Questions: Is There Value in Just One? Paper presented at the annual meeting of the American Educational Research Association and the National Council on Measurement in Education, San Francisco, CA, 6–12 April 2006, p. 6. Available at: http://www.dylanwiliam.org/Dylan_Wiliams_website/Papers_files/DIMS%20(NCME%202006).pdf.

is easy to spot mistakes with a multiple-choice answer and to address the problem immediately.

Elizabeth and Robert Bjork have explored the concept of 'desirable difficulties' to enhance learning and instruction. They explain that students very often have a false sense of confidence about a subject because they have revised by looking over or reviewing their notes.[8] This 'easy' approach to revision makes them feel that they are more knowledgeable and skilled about the topic than is really the case. This is because they have a sense of familiarity about the topic. This sense of familiarity is then confused with deep understanding. Bjork and Bjork (among others) champion testing as a learning approach because 'much laboratory research has demonstrated the power of tests as learning events, and, in fact, a test or a retrieval attempt, even when no corrective feedback is given, can be considerably more effective in the long term than reading the material over and over'.[9] They championed the idea that it is important that students 'make things hard on themselves, but in a good way, creating desirable difficulties to enhance learning'.

A good way to tap into students' need to delve into their memory to recall information, and remember the right processes in order to apply this information, is to include quizzes and tests intermittently across sessions. A challenging multiple-choice question can really clarify how much information has been secured for both student and teacher. However, Bjork and Bjork's concept of 'desirable difficulty' is important here. If things are impossibly hard, the students will be demotivated: 'If … the learner does not have the background knowledge or skills to respond to [tasks] successfully, then they become undesirable difficulties.'[10] The skill is in judging when students are ready for such approaches and how they can be deeply involved in thinking about the learning involved.

---

8   Bjork and Bjork, Making Things Hard on Yourself, p. 61.
9   Bjork and Bjork, Making Things Hard on Yourself, p. 62.
10 Bjork and Bjork, Making Things Hard on Yourself, p. 58.

Appropriate challenge

A colleague uses challenging multiple-choice questions to probe her students' deep understanding of a topic as part of spaced retrieval practice. The students decide on the answer and note down their response, but they must also be prepared to explain their reasoning. It is not possible just to plump for answer C without any thought, just hoping to strike it lucky. Of course, the skill here is in devising quality questions that challenge students' understanding and identify any weaknesses in degrees of comprehension. Asking the students to explain why other answers aren't appropriate is another useful strategy for strengthening their understanding.

On page 86 you will find a high level multiple-choice geography GCSE question (created by V. Lea of Ashlawn School) designed to determine how much the students understand about the topic of growth rates. You can see that both knowledge and the application of specific skills are required to complete this question. It is only when the students have both that they will be successful.

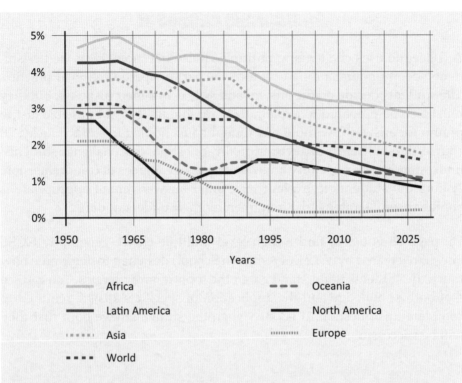

Study the graph showing changes in urban growth rates between 1950 and 2025. Which of the statements below are true?

a. Latin America, Oceania, North America and Europe have below world average growth rates.

b. Europe and Latin America have the largest percentage change between 1950 and 2025.

c. Europe has consistently had the lowest rates of urban growth between 1950 and 2025.

d. Asia and Africa are the only continents to stay consistently above the world average between 1950 and 1985.

The question tests their analysis skills and their ability to read linear graphs that show change. The students must look at all components of this graph in order to answer the question. There is a 'world line' showing the average as well as percentages showing the rate of growth. The students need to do some simple calculations to work out the correct answer and interrogate the graph in a more sophisticated way than they might if they were just describing it – when they might just consider the decline in growth rates, with Africa and Asia having the highest rates overall. Furthermore, there are two correct answers.[11] The students' ability to detect this and discuss the reasons why the other answers are incorrect really pushes their understanding.

Final thoughts

Bjork and Bjork remind us that to be a highly effective learner, 'the basic message is that we need to spend less time restudying and more time testing ourselves'.[12] When we are teaching our classes, reminding them of the usefulness of practice testing – quizzing each other, creating little mini tests and opportunities to learn from the results (particularly the wrong answers) – is one of the most effective and efficient learning strategies available. Of course, the students need to act on these findings themselves. The next chapter on feedback explores this area in further detail.

---

11 Answers (a) and (b) are correct. Although Europe is low overall, its rate of change is a 2% drop and Latin America is 3.2%, making them the two largest changes. The students also need to recognise the world average and understand its importance to get the correct answers. (c) is incorrect because North America records the lowest growth rates between 1965 and 1980; Europe just appears to dominate visually as the lowest – they need to look carefully at the graph. (d) is also incorrect – again, the students need to appraise the dates and data carefully to eliminate this choice: Latin America is also above average for this period.
12 Bjork and Bjork, Making Things Hard on Yourself, p. 62.

Thinking point

- What techniques do you use in lessons to make use of students' mistakes in order to further learning?

- How do you encourage students to self-correct their errors rather than over-relying on you?

- Do your students have a positive attitude towards dealing with their mistakes?

- What teaching activities do you undertake to ensure that foundation knowledge is deeply secured by your students?

- How do you challenge students further with your questioning skills?

- How do you encourage students to think hard about their learning?

- Do multiple-choice questions have a role in your lessons?

- How do you try to encourage students' self-efficacy?

- How do you encourage all students to take part in the learning in the lesson?

Chapter 8
Feedback That Makes Learning Stick

 The first fundamental principle of effective feedback is that feedback should be more work for the recipient than the donor.

Dylan Wiliam

What can encourage us to improve our practice? What can lead to feelings of frustration and hopelessness? The answer: feedback. I have visited many schools and had many detailed discussions with students over the last few years, which has highlighted to me the importance of feedback. This is also reinforced by many research findings, such as work by the Education Endowment Trust which concludes that feedback has 'very high effects on learning' across all age groups.[1]

Good quality feedback gives us clear information about our current achievements and helpful directives about how to improve. Although this sounds straightforward, there are several pitfalls that people fall into when giving feedback. It is worth examining the concept of effective feedback in detail so we can benchmark our own performance against best practice. Feedback is critical in making learning stick because unless we know what we need to do to improve, we are doomed to repeat the same mistakes.

---

1 See https://educationendowmentfoundation.org.uk/evidence-summaries/
teaching-learning-toolkit/feedback.

Who gives feedback?

Feedback comes from several different sources. Most of the time we think of feedback as originating from teacher to pupil, highlighting their success (or otherwise) with a specific piece of work. However, feedback from pupil to teacher is also valuable. Some teachers who solicit feedback from their pupils report that they have found the experience very instructive. It can help them to make their teaching more responsive to their pupils' needs. It also ensures that they are aware of what they need to do to make their lessons highly effective and tells them what is already working brilliantly.

A few teachers explain that it feels 'too brave' to ask for feedback. They fear hearing something negative about their practice. They are also concerned about pupil perceptions being inaccurate or unfair. There are steps that we can take to address this in the way we seek feedback and the questions we ask. Sometimes we can set a task or teach something challenging that our pupils do not enjoy or find immediately accessible, but ultimately it proves to benefit their learning greatly. The following example shows this in action.

In preparation for GCSE mock revision, I used one of the activities in the Toolkit (Silent Debate) with a talented but passive all-girls' class. They were used to listening and working in comfortable friendship groups. At the end of the session I asked them how they had found the new activity, which had demanded a lot from them. They had all engaged and the outcome of the lesson showed great improvements in their skills. However, many of them felt out of their 'comfort zone' because they hadn't enjoyed being individually responsible for their comments. This was unfamiliar to them and it hadn't made for an enjoyable experience. They told me that they preferred to work in their usual groupings and liked to 'depend' on each other. However, the most important question was: had the lesson improved their own skills or not? They admitted that it had (more than any other activity!), particularly because they had been 'forced to think for themselves'.

This experience highlights the importance of asking the right questions, rather than judging success on whether the strategy was enjoyable or not. Learning can be highly effective even when it is not wholly agreeable. It is likely that when we revisit this technique in future lessons, and the pupils become more familiar with it, it will become more enjoyable for them – but this shouldn't be a major driver.

Requesting constructive feedback from pupils is one way that we can all learn more about our practice and ultimately improve. This is supported powerfully by John Hattie's research, which finds that:

 It was only when I discovered that feedback was most powerful when it is from the *student to the teacher* that I started to understand it better. When teachers seek, or at least are open to, feedback from students as to what the students know, what they understand, where they make errors, when they have misconceptions, when they are not engaged – then teaching and learning can be synchronized and powerful. Feedback to teachers helps make learning visible.[2]

As we seek to make pupils more independent in managing their own learning, it is essential that they take an active part in reviewing the feedback they generate for themselves. Pupils need to reflect on their own feedback on their own performance and then use it to make improvements. Pupils are often encouraged to check their own learning and self-test as part of self-study activities. This is useful as they can see what information they can recall easily and which areas require further study, but it is much more valuable if the implications of the feedback are also fully considered by the pupil.

For example, a friend's son had made useful revision cards which highlighted the key information he needed to recall for a forthcoming physics unit test. He tested himself on these cards regularly, but there were some that he always got wrong and others that he recalled effortlessly. He only improved his overall understanding of the topic when he acted on the

---

2 Hattie, *Visible Learning*, p. 173; original emphasis.

feedback the revision activity was giving him – in this case, learning from his persistent mistakes. He started taking the cards he struggled with out of the pack to give them closer attention and asking a peer from his class to go over the process on the card with him so that he could understand the topic better. He also realised that constantly reviewing those areas of the topic he already could recall accurately was not an efficient use of his revision time. It led to overconfidence because he was getting 15 cards out of 20 correct, which made him feel that he was succeeding when he really needed to focus on the five problem areas. His time was better spent dealing with his mistakes and understanding what that feedback was telling him. This enabled him to make the challenging learning stick and ultimately secure examination success.

Six characteristics of quality feedback

Quality feedback in any area of life will have clear characteristics. The following example highlights what happens when one or more of these aspects is missing. As a consultant, I was asked to provide some insight into the challenge facing a history department. They were part of a highly successful school, but the deputy head was concerned that the staff were overworking. Despite the effort they were putting in, the results were less than stellar, particularly with the more able students at GCSE and A level.

During my visit I observed numerous lessons. These were successful. The students were motivated, engaged and willing to participate in all the activities. The lessons had a good pace and effective challenge. Where were things going wrong? When I spoke to several groups of sixth formers, I was surprised by some of their responses to my questions. Although they loved the lessons and aspired to the highest levels of achievement, they were unable to accurately identify what made an exceptional history essay or a great history student. When pushed, they confided that they thought they needed to 'include everything' and make their essays 'really long' to be successful. No wonder their teachers were exhausted!

I realised that even though the teachers were teaching effective lessons, a lack of quality feedback to the students was leading to both their low results and their phenomenal overworking. Recognising that the students' work was below par, they had become trapped in a vicious cycle of setting more and more examination practice, rather than focusing on how to help the students improve areas of weakness. The students had also become overdependent on staff because they didn't share the examination criteria in a way that made success achievable and transparent.

This example highlights the six important aspects of feedback.

1. Feedback needs to be clearly focused on the success criteria for the task

The success criteria should be made available to pupils in a way that they can easily understand. Examination criteria can be impenetrable even to seasoned examiners as it is often jam-packed full of jargon. Writing out examination criteria and mark schemes in 'pupil speak' and discussing the fine detail with them is so important for success. Clarity of expectation is one of the principal ways that success is made more likely.

2. Feedback needs to be prompt

It is easy for pupils' mistakes and bad learning habits to stick if they don't receive timely correction. To be effective, feedback needs to be given as soon after the activity as possible, so the pupils can act on their mistakes before they become deeply embedded. In subjects like PE, performing arts and design, subject teachers are skilled at giving immediate verbal feedback in the moment. However, when 30 pupils are filling exercise books with work, the time delay between marking and giving them useful feedback can be problematic.

Giving feedback to pupils in a timely manner is critical so that they can start learning from it. Conducting a class conference can serve as a practical and time-smart solution, whereby work from a few pupils (perhaps a parallel class) is displayed on the whiteboard using a visualiser and corrected verbally by the class. The teacher then facilitates the feedback by encouraging pupils to give constructive comments about what has been successful about the work – focused clearly on the success criteria. They then have a chance to look again at their own work and make any corrections before it is assessed by the teacher. After all, there are few things more soul-destroying than receiving feedback so late that you have put your efforts in the wrong place and embedded errors deeply into your practice.

3. Feedback needs to be clearly understood and actionable by the recipient

However clear the criteria are, it will still be the case that some pupils will not be able to visualise what this looks like in their work. Being told that they need to 'debate coherently' or 'add suitable analysis' means little unless they can see quality exemplars that show these characteristics in practice. We often ask pupils if they understand what they need to do to improve their work, but we must always be alert to those who parrot back the feedback they receive from us, but don't actually understand what it means at all.

The advice we give to pupils needs to be actionable, and it should be obvious when they have achieved it. The science department in one school conducted some research which showed that if they recorded the suggested improvement advice next to the specific area that needed to be amended, and also posed it as a question, then pupils were more likely to respond and make improvements to their work. The importance of pupil action is highlighted by Dylan Wiliam when he urges: 'If there's a single principle teachers need to digest about classroom feedback, it's this: The only thing that matters is what students do with it.'[3]

4. Feedback needs to be achievable

Pupils can be overwhelmed and demotivated by unclear or overly detailed feedback (on every possible area for development!). It might well be the case that there are countless aspects that need to be improved, but focusing on the top three that would make the biggest difference to the quality of the work is the best way to make this achievable. It is good practice to clearly identify these by pointing to specific examples – for instance, highlighting in which paragraph the mistakes are or showing where further examples could be added.

Getting pupils to focus initially on one (easily fixable) aspect is more likely to result in long-term improvements. For example, perhaps there is a whole section in their history essay that is vague. Asking them to provide at least three other domestic policy examples from other primary historical sources is a good way of helping them improve this area because it is clear, specific and achievable.

5. Feedback needs to be positive and progressive

We need to remember that to motivate anyone to make improvements, we first need to focus on the positives and make improvements seem possible. These positive attributes need to be signalled, so the pupil is clear about what they have achieved and where exactly they have demonstrated these skills. Pupils will be much more motivated to improve if they already feel that their efforts have been noticed and that they are on the way to success.

3   Dylan Wiliam, Is the Feedback You're Giving Students Helping or Hindering? *Dylan Wiliam Center* (29 November 2014). Available at: https://www.dylanwiliamcenter.com/2014/11/29/is-the-feedback-you-are-giving-students-helping-or-hindering.

Highlighting what they have already done well gives them the impetus to want to continue and improve on their ideas. For example: 'The description of Jack's character is very detailed and you explain his role in the novel well. Next, you need to add short quotations to support each of your points.' Here, the follow-up advice is very specific so the pupil won't feel overwhelmed and it is obvious what they need to do next.

6. Feedback needs to result in lasting changed behaviour and improvements

Feedback is a means to improved outcomes rather than an end in itself. It is important that any required improvements are secured not just in a single piece of work but can be readily replicated in future pieces. This is often the trickiest aspect of effective feedback – making those changes translate into new ways of working and making them stick. Students easily slip into old habits, so securing long-term improvements is crucial.

On page 97 is a table that a colleague uses to get her students to record targets from their marked work. That is nothing new. The notable part is that she also asks her students to record where they have demonstrated these improvements in their subsequent work. This is a simple strategy which ensures that students not only take notice of feedback but also take action by persistently practising the desired new behaviour – showing that they can meet the target. This enables the target behaviour to become part of their normal practice and long-term improvements are secured, rather than the student being stuck with the same target for months.

Date	Target	Where met?	Signed off
15 September 2020	Include quotations to support each idea.	*Macbeth* essay (20 September) Poetry timed practice (5 October 2020) Poetry comparison (10 October 2020)	
5 October 2020	Ensure that poetic terms are used correctly.	Poetry comparison (10 October 2020)	

The final word on feedback should go to the researcher John Hattie with this reminder:

 What matters [in improving achievement] are conceptions of teaching, learning, assessment, and teachers having expectations that *all* students can progress, that achievement for *all* is changeable (and not fixed), and that progress for *all* is understood and articulated. It is teachers who are open to experience, learn from errors, seek and learn from feedback from students, and who foster effort, clarity, and engagement in learning.[4]

---

4   Hattie, *Visible Learning*, p. 35; original emphasis.

Thinking point: the feedback square

Each edge of the square below reflects a different feedback track. Each side is important. Consider the questions in the central square and reflect on current practice with one of your classes or groups.

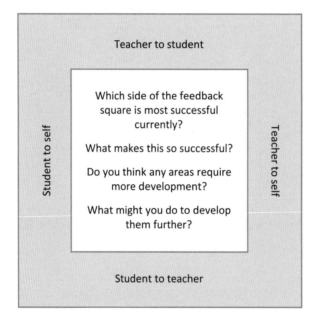

Teacher to student

Student to self

Teacher to self

Which side of the feedback square is most successful currently?

What makes this so successful?

Do you think any areas require more development?

What might you do to develop them further?

Student to teacher

Chapter 9
Peer and Self-Assessment: Why It Matters

> 66 The important leap is when teachers see self- and peer-assessment as unique and highly valuable learning times, which result in students remembering more and having deeper understanding.
>
> Shirley Clarke, *Formative Assessment in the Secondary Classroom* 99

Ask any group of teachers for their views on peer and self-assessment, and how it helps learning, and you will get a very mixed response. Some teachers see it as a much valued and helpful classroom essential. Others, like principal Jo Facer, find peer assessment 'very, very difficult to get right',[1] and suggest that it should be jettisoned in place of more straightforward whole-class feedback (sometimes called 'class conference'). Recent research findings highlight the benefits of effective peer assessment: 'the effectiveness of peer assessment was remarkably robust across a range of contexts' but was 'not significantly different in its effect from self-assessment'.[2]

Observing hundreds of lessons first-hand, I have seen both the amazing contribution that student assessment can make towards securing learning but also the practical pitfalls that need to be overcome for it to be successful.

---

1   Jo Facer, Why Peer Assessment Doesn't Work, *TES* (3 January 2020). Available at: https://www.tes.com/magazine/article/why-peer-assessment-doesnt-work.
2   Kit Double, Joshua McGrane and Therese N. Hopfenbeck, The Impact of Peer Assessment on Academic Performance: A Meta-Analysis of Control Group Studies, *Educational Psychology Review*, 32(1) (2020): 481–509 at 481, 503. Available at: https://www.researchgate.net/publication/337872565_The_Impact_of_Peer_Assessment_on_Academic_Performance_A_Meta-analysis_of_Control_Group_Studies.

Peer and self-assessment gets students involved in reviewing tasks against pre-agreed success criteria. Research by Paul Black and Dylan Wiliam found that 'Assessment by pupils, far from being a luxury, is an essential part of formative assessment.'[3] In my own work, I observe peer assessment much more frequently than self-assessment. There seem to be several reasons for this. Firstly, pairing up students and getting them to reflect on each other's work is much more interactive than sitting and trying to self-assess their own work. This makes peer assessment more engaging because the students know in advance that they will need to assess their partner's work and explain their findings – it gives them a clear focus. Secondly, the activity lends itself to a well-defined structure: discussing the assessment criteria with the whole class to ensure they are clear about what it means, reviewing one another's work by reading or observing, giving feedback verbally and then allocating time for the students to improve their individual work by actioning points for development.

One of the disadvantages of self-assessment is that students often find it challenging to spot mistakes or misconceptions in their own work. There are various reasons for this. Sometimes this is because the errors are so deeply embedded in their practice that they fail to realise that they are in fact errors. (It is often easier to spot mistakes in a peer's work because your eye reads what it expects to read in your own work!) Students have also confessed to me that they are less motivated about reviewing their own work because they know that any improvements they notice will result in additional work for them! The lack of interaction required for self-assessment also means that they often give their work just a cursory glance rather than robustly self-reviewing it against the criteria.

Ultimately, it is the ability to accurately self-review your own work that leads to individual success and independence. I also work as an examiner and when marking students' final pieces it is clear which candidates have checked and improved their work because the workings and amendments are there on the page – the improvements are evident. Students' ability

3   Dylan Wiliam and Paul Black, *Inside the Black Box: Raising Standards through Classroom Assessment* (London: GL Assessment, 2006), p. 10.

to spot a mistake and correct it or reread and improve aspects of their work under examination conditions gives them a massive advantage in examination success. But it doesn't stop there: achieving employment, working and studying successfully at a higher level all depend on the ability to self-assess and improve your first attempt.

The end goal of any teaching must be that the student gains the skills, awareness and motivation to self-assess accurately. This means that they should know their current standard of achievement and be able to self-review, so they are able to reflect perceptively and make any improvements necessary. These are challenging skills to master, which is one of the reasons why peer assessment is so useful. Peer assessment enables students to practise and hone the skills they will need for self-assessment with a partner. This active involvement is key to developing successful learners. Looking in detail at the assessment criteria, checking to see how well the current piece of work meets the criteria and selecting precise areas for improvement demystifies the assessment process and empowers both the student assessor and the peer they assess. Recent research highlights the benefits of peer assessment: 'by performing both the role of assessor and being assessed themselves, students' learning can potentially benefit more than if they are just assessed'.[4]

Student assessment (both peer and self) is a brilliant tool for clarifying the whole assessment process and improving self-regulation skills. However, in some classrooms it rarely takes place. As Facer and others conclude, there are a variety of implementation issues but these can be managed with clear training and setting up an effective feedback structure. In my experience, it is best to secure effective peer assessment first: as the students' reflective skills become sharpened by peer practice, this ultimately helps them to become better self-assessors.

---

4   Double et al., The Impact of Peer Assessment on Academic Performance, 482.

The steps for successful peer assessment

Several steps need to be in place before peer assessment will be successful in improving learning. As teachers, we are often time-pressed and so we rush to get pupils assessing each other without paying sufficient attention to the initial stages. This can lead to unhelpful comments from pupils and improvements to learning that don't stick over time.

To ensure success, think about the following:

1. **Partner pupils up with a peer of similar ability to talk through and review each other's work.** If the ability gap between the pupils is too wide, the feedback process won't benefit either party. The dynamics of the partnership are important too: pupils need to have a respectful and constructive relationship built on trust and mutual support. Close friends might appear to be a good peer pair but they often get distracted into talking about other things or they can feel inhibited about offering areas for development because they feel they are 'criticising' a friend. Setting up effective partnerships takes real thought. The guidelines for conducting peer reviews should be established with the class so they know what is expected of them.

2. **Make sure the class are clear about the success criteria for the work.** My observations suggest that between three and five success criteria is optimum. If there is too much for them to focus on, it becomes difficult to manage and the feedback becomes overwhelming for both giver and receiver.

3. **Demonstrate with the class how to feed back on an anonymous piece of work.** When peer assessment fails, it is often because this vital step has been missed. Modelling what to look for is key, but demonstrating how to give constructive and helpful feedback is also important. The pupils need to develop the skill of focusing on the success criteria, which will help to ensure that their comments are constructive. Even when pupils are well practised at giving feedback,

it can be useful to share with them exemplars of the type of work you are expecting. This means they understand what type of comments are appropriate.

4. **Establish guidelines and protocols with the class about how they should respond to each other's work.** This should include whether they will write on the work and how the feedback should be phrased. Ensure that pupils are specific and give clear examples that describe what they have noticed about the work. Checklists of criteria are invaluable when supporting new peer assessors. These clarify what elements should appear in the work, and the pupils tick whether it has been achieved or not. Recording suggestions on sticky notes is a good way for pupils to provide feedback without writing directly on the work.

5. **Give a clear time limit for the activity.** The pupils should have sufficient time to assess the work and give feedback to their partner. I have found that this takes longer than you might expect, so it is a good idea to watch a few pairs closely to judge when the class have had sufficient time to feed back to each other.

6. **Set aside time for pupils to act on the feedback.** Pupils need an opportunity to record the feedback and amend or improve their work. This is vital because this is when the learning really happens.

Self-assessment

Effective self-assessment is, of course, the ultimate strategy for improving learning and making the changes stick. The stages for supporting this are the same as for peer assessment – but without the peer, of course. Some of the challenges involved in creating effective self-assessment are that pupils are too vague when it comes to setting their own targets and steps for improvement. For example, they may say that they need to 'improve their writing skills' without being specific about how to achieve this.

It is important to build in regular opportunities during lessons to support self-assessment. Successful strategies to do this include:

- **Learning pit stops.** Naturally, pupils want to jump in and get the task done. However, the rush for completion is not helpful in getting them to achieve their best work. Building in breathing spaces – where they stop for five or ten minutes and actively review their work – yields great rewards. Give them extremely specific guidance so they have a precise focus – for example: note down which paragraph of your work is the most effective and explain why; highlight the five best descriptions in your story; identify which section of your performance shows the theme most strongly; underline the aspects of your evaluation which make the most compelling argument.

- **Get pupils to devise the success criteria.** How do we know whether pupils have really mastered something? When they can explain what they need to achieve by constructing the success criteria for themselves. Being able to accurately devise your own success criteria is a huge advantage, whether it is completing an essay on the Russian Revolution or designing a new pencil case.

- **Self-assessment cards.** A colleague has a small index box full of guidance checklists sitting on her desk. When her pupils decide they have completed their work, they select one and then check they have covered all the areas mentioned. The cards are colour coded, so a pupil who struggles with accuracy might be encouraged to take a blue card (which includes reminders about checking work carefully, punctuation and sentencing), whereas a pupil who needs to focus on content might take a yellow card.

- **Reflective journals or learning logs.** These allow pupils to chronicle their progress and reflect on their understanding. One colleague uses these when teaching her primary pupils mathematics. It enables them to consider what they have learned, pose questions and record what they really need to remember about a topic. Another colleague uses them to reinforce new vocabulary: she asks her pupils to remember which new words they have learned that week and then try to use them in some writing. One of the benefits of journals is that they help to develop metacognition – thinking about the learning process. They are also great for helping pupils to see the distance they have travelled with their learning as they can quickly look back over them.

Thinking point

Some useful questions that can be used to prompt these thoughts include:

- The thing I found most challenging about the task was …

- The most important thing I learned was …

- If I were doing this activity again, I would make sure that I …

- What I want to find out more about is …

- What I was most pleased about was …

- What I found most difficult was …

- What I need to remember for next time is …

The Toolkit:
50 Strategies to Help Your Students Remember What You Teach Them

Chapter 10
Sticky Teaching in Practice: Active Classroom Strategies

 It is what teachers get the students to do in the class that emerged as the strongest component of the accomplished teacher's repertoire, rather than what the teacher specifically does. Students must be actively involved in their learning.

John Hattie, *Visible Learning*

Getting sticky in practice

Wouldn't it be wonderful if your pupils remembered what you taught them? The purpose of this Toolkit is to provide a compendium of practical teaching strategies that you can use to help make your teaching stickier and the learning more memorable for your pupils. It is a veritable chocolate box stuffed full of great teaching strategies. Most of them can be easily implemented in the classroom with minimum preparation. Best of all, they will ensure that your pupils are actively involved, rather than you putting in all the effort.

However, the Toolkit comes with a caveat. Although these activities are tremendously engaging for pupils and will help them to secure knowledge and develop their abilities, it is important to select only those that are most relevant to whatever knowledge, skill or information you would like your pupils to master. It is easy to become captivated by new ideas, but unless they are the most appropriate strategies for developing that knowledge or the most appropriate method of helping pupils with that skill, they will not be successful in helping pupils to retain their learning.

Despite this warning, there is a strong case for us to be more flexible and innovative in the way we approach helping pupils to secure learning in our lessons. In my work as a school consultant, I have sometimes suggested a new or different teaching strategy to a member of staff and have been told, 'Oh, I wouldn't like to learn it that way myself' or 'That won't go down well with Year 10', only to find out later that the pupils have loved the technique and proclaimed it massively useful and memorably different!

Of course, as individuals we each have our own favourite methods of learning and revising, but our pupils often need a much wider repertoire to experiment with and select from to ensure their success. As Ronald Gross observes, 'there is no universal optimal method of learning'.[1] As educators we are successful learners; usually, we haven't really had to struggle or actively find strategies to master the subjects we are teaching. It is important that we don't just assume that our pupils will find learning as effortless or automatically engaging as we have. So, have a look at these Toolkit ideas with an open mind and then tailor and tweak them to meet your pupils' learning needs.

Bear in mind, too, that when you use these strategies for the first time there may well be a learning dip (as shown in the diagram on page 111). In fact, I would put money on it! Your lessons may well be running smoothly using your tried and tested teaching techniques, but when you try a new approach it can create confusion and, temporarily, cause the learning to dip and become less successful than it was before.

---

1   Ronald Gross, *Peak Learning: How to Create Your Own Lifelong Education Program for Personal Enlightenment and Professional Success* (New York: Jeremy P. Tarcher/Putnam, 1999), p. xvi.

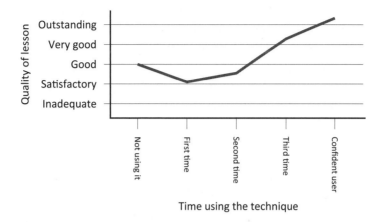

Why failure leads to better learning

The dip in performance can occur for various reasons: perhaps the pupils are unclear about the instructions related to the new technique, perhaps they are resistant to trying out something new or perhaps they are unaccustomed to working in the different pairs or groups required by the new activity. Whatever the reason, it is important not to give up – persistence really matters. Sometimes the task, timings or instructions will need to be fine-tuned to improve the learning. In other cases, once the pupils become proficient with a learning strategy, they will engage with it much more willingly in future lessons. It just takes time for them to build their confidence and realise that, yes, they do have to take part in a different sort of lesson. If an idea doesn't work out straight away, reflect on it and have another go before you jettison it completely. Often, when trying new techniques and approaches, you must hold your nerve and give it a chance to flourish with your class and become part of your established repertoire.

The other key ingredient needed in making learning stick is that the learners are engaged and involved with the learning in the lesson, rather than just being passive passengers. We need a mantra of 'no passengers' and plan our lessons and organise groupings so that all pupils are active participants.

There are dangers in acting as a passenger in any situation that requires you to be able to recall something for yourself. I can remember visiting Manchester with friends three or four times over a period of 18 months or so. We found a restaurant we really liked and would walk to it together from the hotel. If you had asked me if I knew how to find it for myself, I would have said yes, definitely. It was near to the hotel and I had been there multiple times. However, on a subsequent occasion, when I was working in Manchester on my own, I set off to find the restaurant confident that I knew where it was – but it turned out that I didn't! I realised, after getting thoroughly lost, that although I had been there before, I had been so engrossed in talking to my friends that I hadn't taken much notice of how to get there. I had relied on following the group, and this had given me a false confidence about finding my way there when I needed to navigate for myself.

I see this false confidence a lot in lessons and it can fool both learners and teachers. When learners are passive in lessons, or if the lesson allows them to let others dominate discussions, questioning sessions or other activities designed to secure learning, then learning can bypass them. If we adopt teaching strategies which ensure that all learners take part – using their metacognitive abilities, reflecting on the strategy and considering their progress – then success will follow and learning will stick.

Here are some of my favourite sticky learning lesson strategies. As a teacher and adviser, I have tried out many different approaches to find those that make learning stick – often with pupils who have not been the most highly motivated. Some have been adapted from ideas gleaned from the thousands of generous and imaginative teachers I have had the good fortune to meet on many training courses and school visits. They have been trialled and tested in a range of different schools across the country. There are bound to be many techniques here that you can use in your lessons to great effect. Have fun selecting and trialling some out – they will ensure that there are no passengers in your classroom and will help the learning to stick.

1. The Baker's Dozen

This idea is useful for provoking detailed discussion and deep thought. It works well either as an introductory task to a topic or at a more advanced level for revision. It encourages students to look beyond the surface when they are considering a topic.

What to do: Provide an A4 sheet of statements or quotations that will provoke interest or strong opinions relating to the topic being studied. Thirteen statements is a good number to include, hence the name – The Baker's Dozen. These statements should provide enough interest to provoke a lively debate – for example: 'Unification was the best thing to happen to Italy', 'The audience loses sympathy with Maggie by the end of Act 2', 'An artist should never compromise their work to make it more commercially successful'. Students should read through each of the statements and note the three that they find the most thought-provoking. This might be because they agree with the statement, it provokes a strong reaction or because it makes them think deeply. The students should then work in pairs to discuss their ideas, reducing the statements of interest between them from six to two. This will take some negotiation. Then they should join with another pair and as a group of four decide which two statements they found the most thought-provoking. Finally, the teacher should ask for feedback from the groups and carefully explore those that were of most interest by means of a whole-class discussion.

Why it works: Students are forced to decide for themselves which statements they find interesting before they start discussing their ideas with others. This promotes individual thought and responsibility. As the discussion widens, they must still give their reasons and come up with a decision about which statements are of most interest. This intensifies the discussion and encourages them to develop their ideas further. The teacher-led questioning at the end means that interesting ideas can be pushed even further and any misconceptions clarified.

2. Boil It Down

This strategy is a good one to check pupils' understanding of events, stages and sequences. Sometimes pupils muddle up ideas, which makes it hard for them to review their notes successfully. This is a good revision activity to help them boil down the information in a text or procedure into the core components or basic steps.

What to do: Remind pupils that the concept of boiling something down relates to reducing a large volume of liquid or food to its essence. Remind them that it is extremely useful for them to do this as part of their revision – for example, writing down the stages needed to solve a mathematical calculation with several steps (e.g. capture–recapture method). It is also valuable in other subjects – for example, summarising the events that led to the Russian Revolution or explaining what happens in an English literature text. Here is an example from J. B. Priestley's *An Inspector Calls*:

> **Boiling it down: main plot events in Act 1 of *An Inspector Calls*:**
>
> 1. The Birlings are hosting a dinner party to celebrate the engagement of Sheila and Gerald.
>
> 2. A police inspector calls to tell them of a young woman's suicide (Eva Smith).
>
> 3. Greedy Mr Birling sacked Eva Smith from his factory …

Why it works: This activity is useful on two levels. Firstly, reducing things down to their essence and recording them clearly makes for effective revision notes. It is helpful for pupils if they can find reminders easily in their books of key sequences or how to do calculations. Secondly, spending 10 minutes in a lesson asking pupils to boil down, for example, the teleological argument into the five main points (RE A level), when they studied this a few months previously, will help them to see how successfully they remember it. It also encourages pupils to think about the most critical components. They can then check this against their partner's answer – being careful to note any omissions.

3. Gel Pen Challenge

This technique has been used with terrific impact to help students tackle examination questions. Employ it only when you feel that you have already dedicated a reasonable amount of time to teaching a skill – for example, towards the end of a topic or just before a test. This is because the activity is focused on developing students' ability to peer and self-check, as well as honing their examination technique. It therefore depends on them already having a good degree of proficiency in the skills being revised.

What to do: Give each student in the class a different coloured gel pen. (Just giving out different coloured pens will excite some students, so you are already on to a winner in getting them interested!)

First, display an essay question/part of an exam paper that has a question in it that demands a reasonably developed response – for example, a 6-mark science question. Then give each student a sheet of A4 lined paper. Tell them *not* to put their name on the paper – anonymity is crucial here. Remind them of the success criteria required to answer the question effectively. It is a good idea to talk this through – ideally, get them to come up with the success criteria themselves – and check they are confident with this. The students must then work individually on answering the examination question for about 10–15 minutes, or until you have judged that they have made a decent effort in tackling the start of the question. Don't explain why they are using a coloured pen – just get them going on answering the question.

Next, collect the work and redistribute it, making sure that each student gets someone else's work. You will need to exchange work between students of a similar ability. Then give them five minutes to make corrections and improvements to the work using their coloured pen. Has the writer made any obvious errors? How can they raise the level? They are not marking the work – they are amending it with their coloured pen so that it is as accurate as possible or adding improvements to enhance the quality. This might mean correcting a mistake, improving the language or adding extra details that the original student has forgotten. They must then continue answering the question, picking up from where the first student left off, for a further amount of time (about 10 or 15 minutes). They should complete this task using a different coloured pen, so it is clear where their amendments begin. Next, redistribute the work to another set of students and repeat the process.

At the end of the session, reunite the students with their original work, along with its annotations and improvements. I usually lay everything out on a table and ask groups to come up and collect their original piece of work. The entire question will have been completed by several different students, but the most important learning is the reflection and correction that goes on as the work is passed around to different students. Encourage the group to discuss any common mistakes or misconceptions and share good practice. What were they most impressed by? What most surprised them? What corrections were made in numerous pieces of work?

Why it works: Many students make silly mistakes. Peer correcting is a good way of making them more alert to common errors and seeing different ways of improving their answers. The students also get the chance to read a range of different responses. When they realise how the task works – that their efforts will be improved by their peers – they tend to raise their game. The discussion at the end of the lesson really helps to boost students' reflective and metacognitive skills, as they can review where they made mistakes and think about how they will learn from this in the future.

The Gel Pen Challenge is also a highly effective strategy to find out exactly how well your students are doing. Too often, I have found that students are careless when completing examination practice; when I point this out to them, they assure me that they will 'get it right' on exam day. Of course, not checking work properly can become an embedded habit. The fact that their peers spot errors and improve them immediately helps to prevent complacency about test-taking practice. The students automatically start to self-edit and thereby avoid the sloppiness that can cost them crucial marks in the examination hall. It is also an engaging activity because the feedback is immediate. This can be a real win in the lead-up to examinations, as we all know that it can take several evenings to mark a set of test papers. With this activity the feedback is received in the lesson itself!

4. Set the Question: Speed Lines

Involving pupils in setting questions and quizzing each other is not only engaging but informative for both pupils and teacher. Sometimes we can be fooled into thinking that our pupils really understand what we have taught them, when in fact they haven't really grasped it properly. Giving pupils the opportunity to set a question is a good way of getting them to quickly check one another's knowledge.

What to do: It can be a good homework activity to get the pupils to think of three effective questions (and answers) related to a topic. Pupils should design their question and answer towards the end or mid-way through the topic. At the start of the lesson, sit the pupils in two parallel lines opposite each other. They should pose their question to their partner and check their answer. They then swap over and answer their partner's question. When you judge that everyone has answered and posed at least one question (some will manage more), ring a bell or call out 'Move!' Everybody on one side should move up a seat, so they all get a fresh partner, and so it continues. Each pupil will be quizzed by many others. At the end of the lesson, ask for feedback on which questions were the best and which were the trickiest, and encourage class members to explain any issues related to common misconceptions and errors.

Why it works: Pupils enjoy testing one another and it is a good way of seeing just how much they have understood about a topic. Setting a question and an answer demands careful thought. You can encourage pupils to think of tricky questions that will test the topic securely. Moreover, they are more likely to enjoy revising for a test if they know they are going to be active quizmasters themselves!

5. Reading Races and Relays

This idea came from a modern languages teacher who was getting her students to practise completing translations, but it can be readily adapted to other areas of the curriculum. It uses teamwork to motivate students to work together to achieve success. It can be a simple memory activity or it can be used at a deeper level to get them to improve and really think about the quality of a piece of work. It is great as an initial activity to start off a new topic in an engaging way. For example, one primary teacher who was starting a new topic used a diagram of a Viking ship to provoke the interest of her class. It also works equally well as a revision technique for a more complex area.

What to do: The students work in small relay teams, ideally about four or five in a team. All the students within a team are allocated a number from 1 to 5. All number 1 students from each group are allowed two minutes to go up to some text or a diagram displayed on a table. They must study it and try to remember the important details. Then they return to their team and share what it says and how it is presented. The others in the team must scribe, translate or improve it (depending on the nature of the task) on a large sheet of paper – for example, it could be a piece of text in another language to be translated, a complex scientific diagram to be replicated or added to (e.g. key terms could be missing) or a poorly written history essay containing factual errors and poor expression to be rewritten, corrected and improved. Next, student number 2 runs up, studies it and returns to the group, and so on until all the students have taken a turn.

Why it works: The fast pace and competitive team approach appeals to many students. They are tested on looking, remembering and explaining the work to others. The level of challenge can be increased depending on what you would like them to do: merely memorising information is a relatively low-level skill (although it has its place in securing knowledge), whereas transforming a text, correcting subtle errors or adding to a diagram demands a higher level of skill and thought. It is a good task to do to remotivate groups that have lost direction because it is lively and has a clear intended outcome.

You will need to construct the groups carefully to have a good balance of skills. Some 'cool' students are much more accepting of praise when it is given to a group (e.g. 'Well done, Team 2') than when they are singled out for individual attention. Some students have even told me that it doesn't feel like work because it has a brisk, competitive edge to it, and they find it fun. Of course, it is necessary for the students to reflect on what they have achieved, why they recalled only some of the diagram, and review their successes and errors to help them in the future. Each group's work can be compared with other groups' and against the original diagram / text to help with reflection and forward planning.

6. Circuit Training

The inspiration for this activity came from a visit to the gym! The idea of circuit training translates brilliantly to the classroom, particularly for revision purposes. It is ideal for checking and securing skills that you think you have already taught the class. Moreover, even just calling it 'circuit training' gives it the allure of the sports world which I have found to be highly motivating to many teenagers.

What to do: Set up the classroom like a gym with various workstations on different tables. Each station is numbered and has an enlarged part of an examination question or other quick task that you would like the pupils to do. You do need to ensure that the tasks aren't too time consuming (ideally lasting about seven or eight minutes), but they do need to be sufficiently challenging and demand real thought. Tasks that require the short recall of five main points, picking out the odd one and saying why or spotting the three mistakes in a sample answer are ideal.

Pupils should work in pairs of similar ability (so that one of them doesn't complete all the work). This will enable them to discuss and think about their answer together. I also give out a circuit training record sheet (see page 121) for both pupils to fill in while completing the activity. It is useful in ensuring that pupils take the tasks seriously and log their answers.

Start the pairs of pupils at different stations. After the specified amount of time, they should move on to the next workstation in a clockwise direction, completing the activity at each station. It is a good idea to have some hints or prompts on the reverse of the task sheet to aid pupils if they get stuck. Ideally, they shouldn't need to use these.

Circuit training record sheet

Record your answers briefly in the space provided. Award yourself a mark if you get it right. Remember, you learn more from the ones you get wrong! Make a note of any further learning you need to do: what skills do you need to practise to increase your success next time?

Station	Answer	Mark	Issue/learning point
1			
2			
3			
4			
5			
6			
7			
8			

Why it works: It is fun and fast paced. Working in pairs and having a record sheet to fill in promotes accountability because the pupils know that you will go through the answers with them at the end. You could even award a prize to the pair that you think have put in the most effort or made the most progress since the last circuit training session.

The record sheet can be used to promote metacognition, too, which is vital for future progress. If you are clear with the pupils about the skills that are being tested, you can encourage them to reflect on their results. Why did they do better at stations 6 and 7? What was it about station 2 that they found tricky? What skill do they need to work on? You can also gain important feedback about the effectiveness of your teaching. For example, if 70% of the class struggle with the probability questions, then this is an area you will need to revisit and reteach. Encouraging pupils to record learning reflections on their sheet and plan their next actions makes this a great learning experience.

7. What's the Truth?

One of the main challenges of test-taking is securing detailed knowledge about a subject. Part of that challenge is being able to recall knowledge quickly enough in an exam situation. The increased use of multiple-choice questions in some GCSE papers means that pupils can easily mistake the correct answer for one that looks plausibly correct, but isn't. This activity is an engaging way of getting pupils to really understand the key knowledge and root out those 'false friend' answers that frequently trip them up in examinations.

What to do: Give the pupils a list of facts relating to the topic they are studying: 12 should be genuine facts and two should be false. The pupils must debate and decide which facts are true and which are false. They could also create their own 'truths' as an investigative homework: the skill, of course, is in selecting answers that look as though they might be correct but aren't. Alternatively, you can pair up pupils and ask them to come up with a set of 'facts' for different topics and then 'teach' them to the class. The pair that successfully fools their classmates can be awarded points or rewards.

Why it works: The discussion involves a high degree of challenge and participation. As a teacher, you can listen in on their thought processes, which will demonstrate how well the learning has been secured. If pupils come up with these facts or answers for themselves, this will create a higher level of thinking and participation.

8. Tarsia Puzzle Maker

Tarsia is a piece of freely available software which allows you to create a range of puzzles and card games such as jigsaws, dominos and link cards to reinforce key learning with pupils in an interactive way. The cards have questions and answers on each side, and the pupils must find the corresponding answer cards and place them next to each other. This usually results in a shape such as a large triangle or hexagon. Tarsia activities are much loved by maths teachers, but they can be used in a wide range of ways in many different subjects.

What to do: Visit mmlsoft.com/index.php/products/tarsia to find templates. Some of the puzzles on the Tarsia website are already pre-populated with answers and can be simply printed off onto card, cut up and used. Give the cards to the pupils in an envelope and ask them to match the corresponding questions and answers. It is a good idea to get pupils working in pairs so they can have a good learning discussion about the alternative answers.

It is also possible to get pupils to create Tarsias for themselves. Print off a blank Tarsia template and ask the pupils to come up with their own questions and answers. This helps with metacognition because they will need to think carefully about which questions and answers to include. This could be a sufficiently challenging task on its own, or it could be further developed by getting the pupils to cut up their Tarsia and give it to a partner to complete.

Why it works: Tarsias are a brilliant, interactive way of helping pupils to revise key vocabulary or to check knowledge by matching up questions with the correct answers. Pupils enjoy trying to put the different pieces together, and as the cards are moveable they are more willing to reconsider their responses than if they were writing them down. Working in pairs encourages the pupils to discuss the reasoning behind their thinking. The level of challenge is increased when the pupils are tasked to create their own Tarsias.

9. Find the Connection

This is a good activity to help pupils build strong links between the details of a topic, especially for revision purposes. You can use pictures or words as a stimulus, or a mixture of both. The pupils must establish relationships between the different ideas, objects or people and then discuss them.

What to do: Display words or pictures relating to the topic you are revising on the whiteboard or on pieces of card – for example, to find the connection between Henry VIII, Catherine of Aragon, Anne Boleyn, Thomas Wolsey and Hampton Court. The pupils must decide which ones are connected and explain the reasoning behind their order – for example, 'I'm placing Anne Boleyn between Hampton Court and Thomas Wolsey because Anne Boleyn lived at Hampton Court after it was taken from Thomas Wolsey. Thomas Wolsey is linked to Anne Boleyn because he was supposed to help Henry arrange a divorce from Catherine of Aragon so he could marry her. Next, I'm linking Catherine of Aragon to Anne Boleyn because …' And so on.

Pupils can stick these words or pictures into their books and then annotate them to show how much they know or use them to support a detailed written response. Clearly, the more detailed and developed the reasoning behind the arrangements, the better. You can give your pupils specific guidance to stretch them – for example, they must say three things about each card, or, in the case of the historical example, give an accurate date relating to each card. The level of challenge can be increased as appropriate for individuals or groups within the class.

Why it works: Find the Connection can be used to provide quick bursts of activity related to the revision of key information in a way that inspires pupils. It is therefore a perfect retrieval activity. The task can also be completed in pairs or threes so that everyone is involved, or made increasingly challenging by the teacher tweaking the parameters and guidance. The act of discussing the cards and coming up with solutions helps to cement the key learning. The cards also serve as an effective revision aid if they are stuck into pupils' books and annotated in detail.

10. Four-Person Questions

One of the difficulties of ensuring that everybody in class is securing knowledge and learning effectively is managing participation in questioning. Another difficulty is that questioning often only tells the teacher whether or not the student knows the correct answer. Opportunities to clarify answers or dispel misunderstandings are not always as effective as they could be. The use of Four-Person Questions solves these issues.

What to do: Use this strategy to check learning after you think you have taught a skill or when you want to check students' knowledge – midway through a unit is ideal. You can set a question with a single correct answer (e.g. a maths problem) or a more open-ended question that does not have a prescribed right answer (e.g. Which character in *A Midsummer Night's Dream* is the most powerful?).

Place the students into groups of four with one student taking on the role of chairperson (the role should be rotated). All the students should note down their individual response to the question, and then discuss it in their groups and agree on the final 'right' or most popular answer. The chairperson should ensure that each student is given the opportunity to share their response. Those students who have made a mistake should be 'coached' by the group, since they must all be able to explain the reasons for their answer. Even if there is not a technically correct answer – for example, some students might respond by saying that Oberon or Puck is the most powerful character in *A Midsummer Night's Dream* – the discussion about their answers is brilliant for helping all students to develop a well-argued, personal response with supporting details.

Why it works: The set-up means that all students must be involved. The fact that they have to discuss their ideas and come up with one agreed group response also means that factual misconceptions can be addressed. For example, if the answer is 3089, and two people get something different, the 'coaching' discussion behind the error is helpful for clarifying the correct answer and explaining how it was found. Importantly, everyone gets an opportunity to speak. When there isn't one correct answer, this activity is great for ensuring that all the students have a voice and participate by explaining their thinking and championing their own ideas.

11. Stand Up–Sit Down

This is a great activity to ensure that the pupils know the meaning of key vocabulary and demonstrate that they understand important areas. As the name implies, they become actively involved in standing up and sitting down to show this.

What to do: Decide on the specific topic you want the class to revise. Each pupil should think of a key word plus the correct definition and note these down. Everyone should then stand up. A group of three 'expert' pupils are given six minutes to try and remember all the words and definitions they can think of. When each pupil's word and definition has been said they should sit down. The winner is any pupil who has a correct word and definition that the experts have omitted to say.

Why it works: This is an effective activity for reviewing learning, and because it is competitive the pupils seem to really enjoy it. It encourages them to challenge themselves to think of a word and definition that the group of three experts won't remember. The repetition of key words and terms is a good way of getting pupils to remember key information because they will be listening to one another's responses and checking their accuracy. The role of expert should be rotated across the term so that each pupil gets the opportunity to take on this lead role.

12. Be Pointless

This is a variation of the compelling TV game show which requires contestants to think of the right answer to a question. Easy? Yes, but the contestant needs to think of the most obscure and least known right answer to win. For example, if you asked 100 people to think of a James Bond film then some titles would be very well-remembered. These might be classics such as *Goldfinger* or *Octopussy* or the latest film. Perhaps 50 out of 100 people might remember one of these, so you would need to think of a more obscure one – but it needs to be correct. *For Your Eyes Only* might be a winning answer because it is correct and perhaps only five or six people can recall it. This is an incredibly good activity to do with a class because it gets pupils thinking of correct but lesser known answers to questions. It is also useful for teaching key terminology and boosting factual retrieval skills from any area of the curriculum.

What to do: Explain the premise of the activity with the class – that they need to come up with correct but little known answers. You could do a warm-up activity based on something general such as: 'Name a type of food that is sold in the school canteen.' (This activity only works, of course, if there is a definitive list of correct answers.) Set the question and give the pupils a couple of minutes of silent thinking time in which to respond and note down their answers – for example, 'Name part of a flower and its function.' Choose two pupils to be the quizzers and ask everybody else to stand up. The quizzers should think of all the likely answers they can. The other pupils should sit down when their answer is read out. You will find that popular answers (like 'petal' or 'stamen') go very quickly. If the quizzers run out of ideas, they can ask the pupils still standing for their answers. Any other pupils with the same answer should sit down too. The winner is the pupil who has a 'pointless' answer or the answer that is shared with the least number of pupils.

Why it works: Examination success depends on the ability to quickly retrieve knowledge. Learning knowledge or key terms depends on repetition and deep understanding. This is a quick activity that can be slotted into five minutes. It also gives the teacher feedback on what terms or knowledge pupils have at their fingertips and what needs to be embedded further. It does not require any additional resources, so it is a good one to have up your sleeve for a bit of quick but effective consolidation. It is essential to check that pupils fully understand their term by asking them to explain it to the group, rather than them just parroting something without a secure understanding.

13. Wordle

Key terms and vocabulary require frequent reinforcement for students to really cement their understanding of them. Using a Wordle is a simple way to check their comprehension of important terminology, but it can also be used in other creative ways to help make learning stick.

What to do: The free website www.wordle.net/create allows you to create word clouds using key vocabulary relating to a subject or topic. Copy and paste into the website the list of the words you wish to display or use a passage of text. For example, you might want to reinforce terms related to a science topic that the class has been studying. Pasting the words into the Wordle creates an attractive visual display of these key terms. The size of the words corresponds directly to the number of times the word appears in the text (for example, if you want 'photosynthesis' to be the most dominant word, then repeat this word many times). You can change the colours, fonts and layout to create a visually appealing display showing a range of words in varying sizes and colours. Once you have a word cloud you are happy with, you can save it to a public gallery and then copy the link or take a screenshot.

The next time you start a lesson you can display this word cloud on the whiteboard. Give pairs of pupils five minutes to discuss each word, its meaning and how it relates to the topic. The winners are the pair still discussing after everyone else has stopped. It can also be used to start a topic in an engaging way. I saw a modern languages teacher do this recently: the pupils were shown a Wordle full of different vocabulary, then they speculated about it and demonstrated their prior knowledge by already knowing some of the words and making intelligent guesses about others. Word clouds can also be used as colourful and interesting classroom displays related to a topic.

Why it works: Word clouds are very eye-catching. Getting the pupils to speculate and discuss terms in pairs is an effective way of including everyone and getting the whole class thinking. You can include a wide variety of key words and ask the pupils to make connections between them. Perhaps most importantly, it allows the teacher to see how well they have mastered the topic through the points they make. Encouraging pupils to discuss them will highlight which terms might need further reinforcement in subsequent lessons.

Once the pupils are confident with the premise of a word cloud (i.e. the size of the word corresponds to its relative significance), they can be used as an effective plenary. Ask the pupils to create their own word clouds on an area you have been learning about – for example, if you have been studying the topic of erosion in geography, ask them to quickly sketch out a word cloud showing which words they think are most important. Mini whiteboards can be invaluable here because they enable all pupils to quickly respond and show their answers. The real value, of course, comes from asking pupils to explain why they have chosen certain words to be bigger or smaller. This also enables other pupils to consider whether they might have missed out any key terms.

14. Mini Whiteboard or Sticky Note Responses

Sometimes the simplest strategies – such as using a mini whiteboard – are the most effective. One of the best ways of ensuring that there aren't any passengers in your lesson is to require an active response from everyone. The mini whiteboard certainly achieves this with the minimum level of fuss and no extra teacher preparation.

What to do: Students are sometimes daunted by writing things down, so a quick response on a mini whiteboard can be liberating for those who worry about giving the wrong answer or having to provide an extended response. The students can hold up their answers and the teacher can get an immediate snapshot of their understanding. Responding quickly with an answer, some notes or a bullet point plan replicates the rapid thinking and planning required in many examinations.

As well as asking students to answer short factual questions, mini white-boards can also be used to support planning and drafting– for example, planning the five main points they would make in an essay, drafting the opening sentence to a story or sketching out a correctly labelled diagram of the heart.

Why it works: Mini whiteboards encourage direct participation and add to the pace of a lesson. The ephemeral nature of a wipe-off response means that students are more willing to take a risk than they would if they were recording their ideas in their books.

15. Diamond Nine Activity

This is a great activity to promote a high level of thought about a topic or question. Use it when you want to promote debate and discussion or when there is not just one correct answer. Diamond Nine can be used across the curriculum. It is extremely popular with humanities teachers, but I have also trained PE teachers who have used it to teach aspects of fitness, and maths teachers who have used it to get students thinking about which area of the curriculum they find most challenging.

What to do: As the name suggests, students are given nine different cards about an area or topic – for example, the most important reasons why a business might fail in its first year or the most important factors influenc-ing the building of a new housing development. This activity relies on there not being an absolute correct order; rather there are a whole range of suita-ble responses, and the students must justify and provide good reasons for their choice. The students should work together in pairs to arrange these in order from most to least important – as indicated in the following example.

There are various reasons why a business might fail in its first year. List these reasons in order from the most important through to least important.

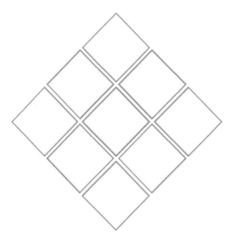

Part of the challenge is that students must follow the format of the diamond shape when arranging their cards. This means they can only choose one top reason and one bottom reason and then select others that are of a similar level of importance for the middle area of the diamond.

Why it works: The discussion the task generates is central to its success. The students must negotiate with one another and come to a joint decision on the order of importance. Some students like to rush through tasks rather than giving them proper consideration. The fact that they can move the cards around, and are actively encouraged to change their minds, is important. This activity relies on there not being an absolute correct order; rather, there are a whole range of suitable responses and the students must justify and provide good reasons for their choice.

Once the pair have made their selection and formed a diamond, there are a number of variations to create additional challenge. These include giving the students several blank cards and asking them to replace some of the least important cards with ones they have come up with themselves. This will promote a higher level of thinking. Alternatively, ask one student to stay with the finished Diamond Nine and the second student to work with a new partner. When everyone is sitting with a different partner, explain that they must either challenge or defend their diamond arrangement. The new partner should ask challenging questions to which their partner should respond. Ultimately, each pair must decide on whether the diamond should stay in its current form or whether they can agree to a negotiated change because of some compelling reason. This modification increases participation and adds challenge because the students will need to champion their own ideas. As a result, they can get incredibly involved and really think about the reasons behind their choices. You can conclude the activity by asking them to return to their original pairs to share their findings with their partner.

16. Silent Debate

This activity is particularly effective for GCSE and A level revision – for example, planning an essay response – but it can also be used for developing extended ideas at Key Stages 2 and 3. It is best completed when you have finished teaching a topic, so remind pupils to revise key areas for the next lesson in order to gain the most from the activity.

What to do: Divide the class into small groups of four or five pupils sitting at separate tables. On each table place a large sheet of paper with a different exam-style essay question or stimulus and a set of coloured pens (one colour for each group). Tell the class that, without speaking to one another (that's the silent bit), they need to respond individually to the question by annotating the sheet (that's the debate bit). After about 10 minutes, they should take their coloured pens and move to the next table, responding and agreeing or disagreeing with the previous group's annotations. Encourage them to add depth and detail to the initial ideas and, where appropriate, debate with other pupils' comments, always making sure that they justify their reasons. It is essential that they complete the task without speaking because they should only be focused on their own contribution.

Why it works: The groups are given different coloured pens, so it is clear which group is trying the hardest to respond to the comments. This also ensures that they each participate effectively. Adding to and challenging one another's comments when they visit a new table and look at the responses that have already been made is a really good way of extending their thinking. Increasingly, the more obvious responses will have been recorded already so they must think of different ways to debate their point. The pupils should be encouraged to add depth and detail to previous groups' ideas and, where appropriate, to debate with others' comments – always making sure that they justify their reasons. There is no escape for those who don't want to participate because they each have a pen and they each need to write a comment – they can't talk to their friends or rely on one person to do all the work.

Although Silent Debate is often used to build ideas and develop arguments for essay plans, it can be applied much more widely too. The initial stimulus could be an essay question – for example, 'Do you think Amazon should pay more tax?' (A level business studies); however, it could just as well be a visual resource for a textiles class or a picture of a historical source.

It is good practice to ensure that the work has a wider purpose. For example, once the Silent Debate is complete, the pupils can return to their original groups and either summarise their findings on the original sheet, discuss some of the best ideas presented by the rest of the class or use the resource as a support to complete a task relating to the debate.

17. Debate Boxing

This is a great way of getting pupils to verbally rehearse their ideas. The idea of contributing to a debate always gets a class interested, and Debate Boxing is fast paced and lively.

What to do: Arrange the class into small groups – five pupils per group is an ideal number because this gives you two pupils on either side of the debate and a judge. Give the class a proposal to debate – for example, 'Euthanasia is always wrong', 'Charles I was responsible for his own downfall' or 'The quality of your diet is more important than the amount of activity you do'. Ask the groups to allocate the roles among themselves: two for, two against and one judge. Give the pairs five minutes of discussion time to come up with some ideas together to support their side of the argument. Then start the debate. The first person on each side of the debate has three minutes to make their argument, followed by the second person. It is useful to have a bell or whistle to manage the transitions. The fifth member of the group should listen closely to the debate and decide which side is the winner. They should make a note of the two best individual arguments made during the debate.

At the end of the debate, you can mix up the groups and restart the debate (give the pupils some time to develop and rehearse the ideas they have heard from the previous team) or set a new topic to debate. It is useful to have a plenary where the judges give feedback on the winning arguments and provide some tips for future debates. It doesn't have to be a typical debate topic; it could be prompted by a discussion about which piece of music is most evocative, which poem is the most effective or which design fulfilled the brief most successfully. Alternatively, it could be more controversial: 'Hurricanes are a more dangerous natural hazard than earthquakes' or 'Van Gogh is a better artist than Claude Monet'.

Why it works: Pupils get extremely excited by the idea of debates and doing it in this structured way gives you a level of control and organisation. Every pupil has a clear role which means they all have to engage. You can also make decisions about which pupils are for or against the proposal and arrange the groupings to which help with differentiation. Verbal rehearsal is a good way for pupils to cement their ideas about key issues and, of course, they will be more successful at debating if they have a better and more refined knowledge of the topic. It can be interesting to hold a debate at the start of a topic and again towards the end to see how their ideas have changed and progressed. We often ask pupils to jump straight in to writing essays about unfamiliar issues, but a verbal discussion is a useful way of getting them interested about writing and developing their ideas. The contribution of the fifth member of the group means they receive immediate feedback on their stance and how they can improve.

18. Thinking Continuum

This is a dynamic and interactive way of getting students to reflect on a controversial topic or to come up with their own judgements. It also encourages them to support their ideas.

What to do: Share a statement with the students at the heart of a topic they are currently studying – for example, 'Napoleon's domestic policy strongly benefited France' or 'How far do you feel sympathy for Othello in Act 5?' The students should arrange themselves in a line showing to what extent they agree or disagree with the statement. Once the students have selected their position you can start a discussion. You can add extra information and see whether this would influence their decision – for example: 'If Desdemona hadn't actually died at the end of the play, would this influence your response?' The Thinking Continuum can also be deployed at the start and end of a lesson to see whether the students' views have changed. The activity works particularly well to get students ready to answer essay questions. It is important to give them sufficient time to develop their thinking.

Why it works: This activity is successful because it gets the students out of their seats, and because everybody is involved, the views of the whole class are represented. All the students must think for themselves and you can also call on individual students to defend their ideas.

19. Quiz in Six

Getting students to record the essentials about a topic is a good way of cementing their learning. Moreover, if the essence of a topic is distilled and written down on small cards (about the size of your palm), this can help students to think carefully about the key information they need to learn and understand. Using the cards to test each other is an effective retrieval exercise.

What to do: Explain to the class that they will be making a set of revision cards to remind them of key learning and as a way of testing each other about their knowledge. Display a colourful example with some key information about a topic on the whiteboard. It should have a clear heading and feature six important pieces of information. For example, camera functions (for GCSE photography) might include portrait mode, self-timer, depth of field, aperture, exposure and shutter speed, and explain why they are used.

The information can be presented in various ways, such as bullet points or labelled diagrams – whatever the student decides is most appropriate in helping them to learn. They must then devise six related questions and write these on the reverse of the cards.

Once the students have created their cards they should work in pairs to select a card from either their own pack or their partner's. Give them five minutes to study the information displayed on the front of the card (thereby refreshing their memory). When the time is up, they should give the card to their partner, who should ask them for a number between 1 and 6 (or they could roll a die) and then read out the relevant question from the back of the card. This exercise can be repeated several times until they have answered all of the questions from the card or, alternatively, a new card can be selected from the set.

Why it works: In order to make the cards, the students need to distil essential information from a topic to its main points. Deciding what these are by reviewing their notes makes this a good revision exercise. The students are also tested on their partner's cards which are likely to contain different information to their own, thereby making the revision more thorough. Encourage the students to note down which questions they found problematic so they can focus their revision on areas of weakness.

20. Doughnut Reading Round

Some readers might be familiar with this great technique from my book *Raising Achievement Pocketbook*.[2] It is a fantastic way to ensure that students read and understand the text or required reading on a topic.

What to do: You will need to demonstrate this technique with the class the first time you use it, so they understand how it works. Set a piece of reading for homework – this could be a chapter in a textbook, an article, source, poem or even a diagram. Divide the class into small groups of four or five students. Each member of the group should prepare between five and ten questions for the group to answer related to what they have read. These might be genuine questions to elicit a better understanding or questions posed to provoke a debate and deepen thought. Each person should ask one of their questions to the rest of the group – for example: 'Is it a primary or secondary source?' 'What year did the Northern Rebellion start?' 'What implications did the Northern Rebellion have for Queen Elizabeth I?' 'Is this a more reliable source than the diary entry?' Each person in the group should answer the question and then pose one of their own questions.

Why it works: Sometimes students don't complete assigned study and sometimes they read things without really thinking or absorbing it. This activity prevents both of these problems. Moreover, having to devise

---

2   Caroline Bentley-Davies, *Raising Achievement Pocketbook* (Alresford: Teachers' Pocketbooks, 2015), p. 112.

questions themselves means they have to think about the resource carefully. The fact that questions are posed to and discussed with their peers enables them to seek clarification about any areas on which they are unclear. To create varying levels of challenge you can guide them towards devising different types of questions – as the next technique demonstrates.

21. Keep Your Gold Coins

This idea comes from Lesley Ann McDermott, a history teacher from north-east England. It helps to solve the common issue of pupils not taking time to check or correct their work.

What to do: Before pupils hand in their work, they must check it against the success criteria for the activity and look for common mistakes. For example, if they have been explaining the reasons behind the murder of Thomas Becket, then one of the success criteria might be to include the key details, dates and the names of the people involved. Another might be to write in clear sentences using correct punctuation. The pupils check their work and should make any necessary corrections. The work should then be given to a partner of similar ability to check. Each pupil has a notional 10 gold coins (or even some 'gold' plastic ones!): for every mistake that should have been corrected, one coin is deducted. They must record at the end of the piece of work how many coins they have left. Pupils often draw little coins on their work (or use plastic ones) to demonstrate losing a coin. For each coin that is lost they should write down next to it why this was – for example, writing Thomas with a small 't' or recording an incorrect date.

Why it works: Pupils are keen not to lose any of their gold coins through silly mistakes, which means that they check their work much more carefully so that it represents their best and most accurate work. This reduces the number of careless errors, thereby allowing the teacher's written assessment to focus on more serious misunderstandings rather than correcting things the pupils should have spotted for themselves. Encourage your pupils to keep a tally of how many coins they have retained from each assignment, as this will help them to see that they are making progress.

22. Space in the Lift

This idea is a fun one to get the students thinking deeply about why a person or feature is important. It requires them to visualise a lift with limited capacity, such as in a hotel or other tall building, and decide who or what merits a place.

What to do: Explain to the class the premise of the group activity. Each group will be given one aspect or person from a topic they have been studying and they must defend why it or he/she deserves one of the few spaces in the lift. In other words, why is that specific person or thing important? This could be a fictional character (e.g. the most important character in *An Inspector Calls*) or an aspect/feature (e.g. the most effective strategy when marketing a new business).

Place the students into small groups and give each group a different character/feature to defend. They must undertake some research (by consulting books or other materials), gather their ideas and then discuss as a group why their person/feature is the most important. Now, redistribute the groups so that each student is in a new group where they should each take it in turn to defend their original group's choice. Encourage the groups to allow each individual time to discuss the ideas related to their individual/topic. They should then decide which person presented the most compelling reason and report back to the rest of the class. If necessary, the groups can decide this by a vote (not voting for themselves, of course!). The winners are the groups whose character/feature is given a space in the lift. A profitable whole-class discussion can help to probe the reasons behind the selections further and fill in any gaps in knowledge.

Why it works: Students become very invested and competitive when defending their allocated person/concept. This motivates them to find effective reasons and explain them thoroughly to their peers. They are initially supported in generating and discussing ideas by working as a group who are all considering the same topic. However, the main part of the activity is championing their own viewpoint, as this helps to develop their independence and self-confidence in preparation for completing any follow-up written work.

23. Question Stems

Getting pupils skilled in asking questions encourages them to think carefully about a topic. They enjoy designing short test papers and quizzing each other using questions they have created, although they often need guidance in designing good questions.

What to do: Give out a detailed resource – this might be a diagram, picture or piece of text. Ask the pupils to study the question stems on page 142 (I have these laminated on a strip like a bookmark). Every pupil must come up with a question for each of the five areas. They can then use the questions to quiz each other. Alternatively, the questions can be recorded on individual slips of paper which you can collect in and redistribute among the class. They each then have a new question to answer.

Why it works: Designing questions taxes pupils' metacognitive skills – they must really think whether a question is good or not. It is often much more demanding to think of a question rather than just answer one. This is because they must first study the whole resource before they can decide on the question. Asking them to provide a range of questions matching the question stems also increases the challenge. Pupils also love being in the role of the teacher for a change!

Knowledge questions	Comprehension questions	Applying questions	Exploring questions	Evaluating questions
What did ...?	Why did ...?	How can you use ...?	What if ...?	Compare/ evaluate/ justify ...
When did ...?	What are the main points?	How would you change ...?	Consider ...	How could you defend ...?
Who did ...?	What does this mean?	Can you apply X to Y?	Think about ...	Decide which example you think is the best and explain why.
Which word means ...?	Why has X been used?	Can you use this information to help you?	Discuss ...	How could X be better in your work because of Y?

24. Defining Moments

Many students come unstuck because their recall of key terminology is insecure – and, of course, they must have it at their fingertips in the examination. This strategy helps with this problem. It is a good way to start a lesson because it reminds students of these key terms, supports their writing and helps them to answer exam questions.

What to do: Arrange the students into pairs of similar ability. Give each student an A4 sheet of paper and ask them to divide it up into boxes – four down and four across (16 sections in total). They should then note down some key terms from the topic in the boxes in the first column and leave the second column blank, which they will then fill with the definitions of those terms. In the third column they should record some additional terms, with the final column again left blank for the entry of these additional terms' definitions. The pairs should then swap papers. The partners should write down their definitions/words in the blank columns. The answers are then returned to their partner to check for accuracy. Finally, any tricky issues can be discussed with the whole class. Below is a part of an example from Year 9 mathematics on the topic of probability.

Word/term	Definition	Word/term	Definition
Mode	The number that occurs most often	Mutually exclusive	
Mean		Relative frequency	
Bar chart		Venn diagram	A diagram that uses circles to show relationships between different sets of data.
Median		Denominator	

Why it works: This activity has a good pace because you can set a time limit. Everybody gets involved and there are clearly correct answers. All the students will see the value in learning these key terms and it is a useful way to look at those that are causing any issues. If students are moving on to extended pieces of writing or creating questions for themselves, then this activity really reminds them of the essential terminology and the need to use it correctly.

25. Mind the Roadworks!

This activity is a good one for getting pupils to think about what aspects of a topic they find tricky. It reminds them that there are common mistakes and areas of challenge and that they need to be alert to them.

What to do: Display five outlines of road signs, such as the hexagonal stop sign, warning triangle and no entry circle. Explain to the class that road signs like these are used to warn or remind drivers of hazards on the road. Likewise, within the topic they have studied there are areas that pupils find tricky or where common mistakes are made – for example, in biology, many pupils think that respiration just means breathing out, or they get the literary terms simile and metaphor mixed up in English, or radius and diameter confused in maths. Give the pupils a few minutes to think of five common mistakes in the topic you have studied. They should then work in pairs to share these and record under each sign an effective strategy for dealing with the mistake.

Why it works: The ability to reflect on likely mistakes and common misconceptions is essential to examination success. If pupils can become skilled at predicting what these errors are, and find strategies to avoid making them, their work will improve. Thinking about different strategies to solve mistakes in this way develops their metacognitive abilities as it gets them thinking about the learning process. It is also motivating because it shows pupils that there are practical steps they can take to make their work more accurate and to avoid dropping marks.

Chapter 11
Sticky Teaching in Practice: Plenaries

Plenaries are useful for many reasons. There are various definitions, but mine is that a plenary is allocated time to allow pupils to review and feed back on what they have learned. A good plenary is invaluable for both pupils and teacher: the pupils get to demonstrate their progress, ask questions and reflect on what they have learned, and the teacher gets an opportunity to see what they have mastered, what still needs to be developed and where to go next.

Plenaries are also valuable in securing learning – they are a quick way of 'testing the temperature' so that misunderstandings can be clarified – and it is for this reason that great teachers don't always leave plenaries until the end of the session. I have observed countless lessons where a superficial review has taken place in the last five minutes, leaving insufficient time to explore misconceptions. When this happens, the plenary becomes tokenistic, something bolted on to the end of the lesson rather than adding to the learning. It was clear during some of these observations that the pupils had stopped making progress midway through the lesson, and it would have been much more helpful to have reviewed the learning much earlier, so the teacher could adjust the lesson and fill in any gaps in understanding.

Sometimes you will want your class to take a 'learning pit stop' or reflection point midway through a lesson to evaluate how their learning is going. This might be particularly important if they have been working independently for some time or have completed a large amount of work in the previous lesson. It allows you to check in with them to see how much progress they are making, clarify key areas or refocus certain pupils. At other times this won't be necessary – effective questioning and 'working the classroom' as the lesson unfolds will ensure that you are clear about how well they are doing. In this case, stopping them will not be the most effective use of their time. You are the best judge of when it is most appropriate and what plenary activity is best suited to reviewing the learning.

A brilliant IT teacher shared a useful tip during one training session. She told me that her pupils were always very keen just to 'get on' with the current project or piece of work. She realised that this urge to get on meant they were often rushing through their work and weren't reflecting on what they were doing or what qualities it needed to show to be successful. She also realised that she too was guilty of wanting to push her class on to the next thing, rather than providing time for meaningful reflection. She now periodically shares a slide of a giant red 'pause' button in her lessons to remind her and the pupils of the need to pause, reflect on and review their work. Making time to show the slide and allowing pupils the opportunity to review their assignments – referencing back to the success criteria or discussing their progress with another pupil – is time well spent and so valuable in improving the quality of work.

A plenary should give you the chance to see what the pupils have mastered and what still needs to be developed. Don't be afraid to ask, 'What three things have you learned today?' but also, 'What do you still need to consolidate?' Sometimes we can be too keen to hear what has gone well, but finding out what still poses a challenge may be more fruitful in securing the learning. Make sure to note down the pupils' responses and then clarify and revisit any problem areas that they haven't yet secured, even if you need to dedicate time at the start of the next lesson to fully consider this. The best plenaries also promote metacognition. They don't just give the pupils an indication of how well they have done; they also involve them in thinking about the learning process. What made them successful? How can they learn from this for next time?

There is a clear overlap between effective teaching strategies and good plenaries. Many of the teaching ideas in Chapter 10 can be tweaked to create an effective plenary, but here I have suggested some additional methods for reviewing that you might like to add to your toolkit. It is always worth ringing the changes with pupils so that plenaries don't become too predictable. Some of these will be ideas you already use, some may have dropped off your radar and are worth revisiting, and others will be new to you. Like any teaching strategy, some will be better suited to your pupils and the subject context than others. Here are 25 purposeful plenary ideas you might like to try.

1. Odd One Out

This is a straightforward but effective way of finding out how much has been mastered during a topic. Display three things on the board – these can be words, pictures or equipment. The students must decide which one is the odd one out and explain why. It is the thinking process rather than the 'right' answer that is important here. Odd One Out is an interesting way to conclude a lesson as it can bring together key areas from the topic as well as checking that the students' understanding and use of terms is secure. It also allows them to make thought-provoking observations and connections.

2. Double Wheel of Knowledge

The students must generate a question linked to the topic you have been studying. You can hand out pre-prepared questions on cards, but I prefer to ask them to make their own as part of the review process. The students stand in an inner and outer circle with the same number of people in each ring. The students in the inner circle face each person in turn and ask their question and then answer their partner's question. They then move one place in a clockwise direction so they are facing a new partner; the students in the outer circle do not move. This is a dynamic way of checking knowledge and ensures that everybody is involved.

3. Colour Chart Plenary

Paint colour charts from DIY stores make for a colourful and engaging way to make pupils think deeply about a topic. This strategy is most applicable when there are multiple answers and when you want the pupils to think hard about their responses – for example: 'What are the most important reasons why the Parliamentarians won the English Civil War?' (A level history) or 'What are the most important ingredients in a ghost story?' (Year 5 English). Starting from the bottom of the chart, ask the pupils in pairs to fill it up with as many good ideas as possible; I often give them a basic answer at the bottom of the ladder to start them off. Pupils tend to think of the most simple or obvious answers first, so the ladder is a visual way of encouraging them to think more deeply about the issue and come up with their best or most suitable answer. Asking pupils to complete these in pairs of similar ability can create some appropriate competition across the classroom.

What follows are two colour chart plenaries (featuring two completed examples) – one from A level history and one from primary English.

A level history

Complete the chart showing the top six reasons you think were most important in accounting for the fact that the Parliamentarians won the English Civil War.

Once you have completed this, find another pair and discuss your ideas. The top one needs to be the most important.

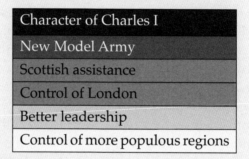

| Character of Charles I |
| New Model Army |
| Scottish assistance |
| Control of London |
| Better leadership |
| Control of more populous regions |

Primary English

Complete the chart showing different words to describe the character of the fox in Roald Dahl's *Fantastic Mr Fox*. The best one should go at the top. Use a dictionary to check the meaning of the words and be prepared to explain the reasons for your answer.

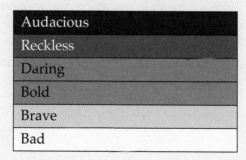

| Audacious |
| Reckless |
| Daring |
| Bold |
| Brave |
| Bad |

4. Quiz, Quiz, Trade

This interactive plenary involves pairs of students quizzing each other and swapping question cards. It is possible to make a set of cards yourself, but I find it really helps to embed the learning if the students make them for themselves. You can get the students to devise their own questions as homework. The card might have a picture or diagram on one side and some follow-up questions on the other side.

The cards are intended to pose a question and then probe the students' understanding to really test their knowledge. For example, a card for GCSE RE might feature an image of part of a church, such as the font, which the student is expected to name. If they give the correct answer, the questioner goes on to ask them for more information – for example, 'Can you tell me more about the function of the font in a church?' This encourages them to give as much information as they can – ideally, the full answer is on the card. If the student misses out or forgets anything, the quizzing student should help them to remember by prompting them. If they still can't think of the right answer, they should be told the answer and should think about how they will try to remember it in the future.

The students must circulate and quiz their classmates. Once they have asked each other their questions they can swap or 'trade' the cards. Then they go and quiz another person with the new card. This is a fast-paced way of checking the learning that has gone on: you can stand back and observe progress and it is fun for the students. The fact that they have to quiz one another is helpful for securing their own knowledge. This is a useful activity for cementing knowledge about key terms and expanding the depth and detail of students' understanding about a topic.

5. Traffic Lights

Ask the students to rate and traffic light (red, amber, green) their degrees of competency relating to the specific criteria involved in a topic or piece of work. In order to make this meaningful, don't simply allow them to mark something green if it is easy or red if they are finding it difficult; rather, encourage them to annotate their ideas and explain why they feel confident or why they are having trouble grasping it. This activity gives the students permission to signpost any gaps in their knowledge, and thereby gives you the feedback you need to help them fill in those gaps.

It is not desirable for all the students to mark items as green either, as this suggests that the task hasn't been challenging enough. Students are well versed in telling teachers what they think they want to know, so make sure that you ask learners who highlight something as green to explain and justify exactly what they know. This will ensure that they genuinely have secured a deep level of understanding rather than just saying they have.

6. Grid and Go

This is an effective and lively way of getting pupils to check each other's learning. Give each pupil a grid (an A4 piece of paper divided into boxes – I usually go for four across and three down, giving 12 boxes, but you can opt for more). You can pre-populate each box with a question or leave some blank and ask the pupils to come up with some questions themselves – which will, of course, promote deeper thought.

Initially, give them five minutes to answer a maximum of three questions. This will give them the opportunity to demonstrate what they already know. Then they should circulate and quiz their classmates about the remaining questions, writing the person's name in the box if they give a correct answer. To ensure the process doesn't take too long, you can award prizes to the pupil who completes the first two rows (like bingo)!

Grid and Go makes for a really useful learning activity, especially if it is followed by an opportunity for the class to reflect on which questions they found challenging (and why), which questions were too easy, which were really worth asking and how they would change their approach if they did it again. Of course, it is crucial that students actively reflect on the questions they found difficult and plan what action they will take to ensure that they learn from the activity.

Below is an example of Grid and Go from a lower school science class on the topic of plants.

Grid and Go – Science

Complete up to three squares with answers yourself, then circulate and ask people from different tables for their answers. Come and see me when you have completed two rows. Don't forget to fill in the person's name and note down their answer in brief.

Why are the leaves of plants green?	Name three things that can limit the rate of photosynthesis in plants.	Where does photosynthesis take place?	What is chlorophyll?
Why is oxygen produced in the carbon cycle?	Where do plants absorb water? *Through their roots.* *Ben P.*	Some glucose is used for respiration. What happens to the other glucose?	What happens in photosynthesis if the plant gets too cold?

		Converted to starch. Holly B.	
Why might plant growers use artificial light?	What does the 'photo' in photosynthesis mean?	What happens if there is not enough water for the plant?	Name two minerals plants need in order to grow well.
If a plant is stunted in growth, which mineral is missing?	If a plant's leaves have turned yellow, what is it deficient in?	Where would a plant get water from?	What is respiration?

7. Tweet It or Facebook Status

Ask the students to 'tweet' or write an imaginary Facebook status about what they have learned in the lesson. What would the tweet include? Not only is this a quick and effective way of summarising ideas, but it also helps you to ascertain whether the students have really identified the most important aspects of the learning. Limit them to a specific number of words, such as 10, to really focus their minds. These can be completed on sticky notes and stuck on the door on the way out of the lesson. It can also be useful to get them to record the tweet in their books for future reference, perhaps using a different coloured pen. The summary can be helpful for revision purposes as it serves as a reminder of key learning from that lesson in snapshot form.

8. Snowball Plenary

First, ask each student to record individually their ideas connected to a 'big' question or topic. This is useful as they are having to think for themselves. For example, when revising natural hazards in Asia for Year 9 geography: 'What are the key things you can remember about this topic?' or 'What aspects of this topic do you think others might forget?' Next, ask them to share their ideas in pairs, adding to and enhancing their answers. They then move to a larger group (four or six students is ideal) to come up with the best answer, which is shared with the wider group. This activity is a good one because everyone must get involved and the sharing and discussion involved in each stage of the task really gets the students thinking.

9. Scan or Use a Visualiser or Camera

Use the plenary as an opportunity to share some good work or highlight effective practice you have found in the lesson. Ensure that all the pupils can see it by scanning it and/or using a visualiser. Ask the class to respond critically (but supportively) by picking out what works well and what could be improved. This avoids the 'mumble and then read out' plenary, which can be both dull and a waste of time because class members can't really evaluate the work because they can't see it.

10. Change It

For this activity, the students are required to change the format that information is displayed in from one type to another – for example, a diagram becomes a piece of prose or instructions become a pictorial diagram – to help reinforce and embed key knowledge. In order to do this successfully, they must really understand the essence of what they have studied. If the students complete this activity in pairs, the discussion they have will be valuable in cementing their understanding.

Change It can also be a physical activity: a process can be spilt up into sections and the students can freeze-frame them (essentially use their bodies to create a still photograph of the key point). Although this sounds straightforward, it depends on close study and a good level of understanding.

After the students have completed their transformation, the pairs or groups can circulate to see which of their peers have presented it most successfully and reflect on any common issues or challenges. The discussions that take place are invaluable for clarifying key learning points.

11. Catch, Think and Say

One student has a beanbag and they must come up with a question or pose a statement that someone else must answer, add to or agree with. For example, the first pupil could say: 'One of the effects of earthquakes are fires. Can you explain why … Toni?' and throw the beanbag to Toni. Toni needs to respond and then pass the beanbag to somebody else along with another question: 'What's another after-effect … Carl?' Alternatively, the teacher can come up with the initial question – for example: 'Give one way that crime negatively affects society … Amara.' This is a useful plenary activity because it requires the students to be quick thinking and can efficiently revise the key learning from the lesson. Although only one pupil will catch the beanbag at a time, all the pupils should be ready with an answer and a question because they don't know who will be selected next.

12. Three Questions

If you are explaining something and want to ensure the students have understood it fully, get them to note down three questions they would like to ask. They should then circulate for 10 minutes asking each other their questions, and afterwards share the findings in a class discussion. Which questions were most frequently asked? Which questions did the students find to be the most challenging?

13. Peer Teaching

Organise the class into small groups of three or four pupils and ask them to 'teach' one of the key parts of the unit as revision for the rest of the class. They should try to think of imaginative ways of presenting the information – for example, creating a quiz or preparing a supporting hand-out to really help them focus on what they think are the key parts of the topic. Give them a limited amount of time to prepare (it makes an effective homework activity). The groups then have five or ten minutes to deliver their presentation. The pupils should be peer marked by their classmates on their effectiveness, clarity and whether they have helped the class to retain the key information. Dividing up the topics so that everybody is responsible for a specific area is an effective way of making sure that everyone is accountable.

14. Make the Link

This task requires the pupils to not only recall information but also relate it to previous learning – for example, 'In what ways is King Louis XVI's domestic policy like Charles I's?', 'How is Buddhism similar and different to Judaism?', 'What are the similarities between two materials/tools/ideas?', 'Give me five similarities between the geography of China and New Zealand.' Questions like these encourage deeper thinking and prompt the pupils to really analyse each area.

15. Three Things I Know – What's Next?

Ask the pupils to record three things they know and then ask them what they would like to know next. Giving them five minutes to discuss their answer with a partner is useful not only in improving the quality of their responses, but it also gives them an opportunity to rehearse and clarify their ideas. Discuss the questions as a class and see if anyone can answer them. Alternatively, you could create a question wall where the pupils can note down any questions they would like answered. It can make an effective start to another lesson to get pupils to answer the questions set by their peers. Remember to ask them how they will try to make the answer stick for the future.

16. Here's the Answer – What's the Question?

Write down some key words or facts from the lesson on the board, such as names, dates, places or whatever is most appropriate to the topic. Ask the pupils to make up a question related to the word or concept. For example, if you wrote 'Tomatoes' on the board, the answer might be, 'What is a rich source of vitamin C?' or 'What might be a key ingredient in a Mediterranean vegetable sauce?' It is usually possible for there to be a range of questions, so it really makes the pupils think. They can then discuss which questions are the most interesting and check whether they are correct.

17. Task and Show

Give students a mini task to complete that will exemplify what they have learned in the lesson. For example, if they have been learning how to describe the poetic techniques in Seamus Heaney's nature poetry, show them a different poem about nature (either by Heaney or another poet – for example, Ted Hughes) and tell them they have five minutes to explain the techniques used in three sentences to the person next to them. The idea of the mini task is to quickly condense and transfer knowledge about what has been learned in the session. This strategy also works well for subjects like art and design and technology.

18. Best Explanation

Write down some key vocabulary from a topic on slips of paper and pop them in an envelope. Ask each student to pick out a word and then write down an explanation of the term in their own words. They should then swap their word with someone else's and try to add to or refine their definition. Can they see anything that is missing? Can they improve it? The class should then discuss any of the words they found problematic to explain, consider which definition is the best or whether any vital information is missing.

19. Teach It to Me!

Ask pairs of students to devise a quick starter activity that will demonstrate whether their peers' learning is secure. This task not only highlights any gaps in their own knowledge, but the creativity involved in designing it also helps to fix the learning in their minds. Working in pairs means they can think through and discuss their responses. Over a period of weeks, arrange for the pairs to 'teach' their mini starters to their peers. This is a perfect retrieval activity and, spread out over time, will really help to make the knowledge stick.

20. What If?

Getting the students to ask speculative 'what if' questions really pushes their subject knowledge by prompting them to imagine likely consequences and explain their thoughts and reasoning. For example, 'What if the French government had not been deeply in debt in 1789?', 'What if the VAT rate were decreased?', 'What if potassium were added to the formula?'

21. Word games

Quick word games can help pupils to demonstrate their knowledge and provides an opportunity for you to spot and unpick any misconceptions. Pictionary, Taboo and Just a Minute (talking about a topic without hesitation, deviation or repetition) are all great ways of testing and securing knowledge and key vocabulary. Word games don't demand any excessive preparation, so they can be squeezed into a session when an opportunity arises.

22. Make It Memorable

Give the pupils opportunities to use diagrams, pictures, mnemonics or rhymes as a way of remembering key systems or information. This encourages them to think hard about the topic and distil the most important aspects. You could also give out play dough or a set of blocks, Lego or coins to pupils and ask them to create an image or diagram to reflect the key learning point. Then ask them to explain it to their partner to help to fix the learning in their minds.

23. Traffic Light Challenge Quiz

Give pairs of pupils six sticky notes: two each of three colours (green, orange and pink). Ask them to devise six questions on the topic they are revising and record one question on the front of a sticky note and the corresponding answer on the back. The questions should have differing amounts of challenge: green should be easy questions, orange slightly harder and pink really hard. They should initial the front of each sticky note so it is clear whose questions are whose. These should be stuck up on the wall or board. It may be useful to have some pre-prepared questions too.

Each pair of pupils should now buddy up with another pair to form a four and work as a team to decide which questions to answer. They receive one mark for a correct green question, two for an orange and three for a pink. They must select several sticky notes to answer (they shouldn't select their own!). The winning team is the one that picks and answers the highest number. You can make it more challenging by telling them they need to score a certain number to win (e.g. 21).

Pupils love the competitive nature of the task, without realising that designing the questions deepens their learning and develops their metacognitive skills, since they must also decide which questions are at which level of demand. It is useful to allow them to access their study notes when they are formulating their questions.

24. Photo Progress

Jo Baker, head of art at Branston Community Academy in Lincolnshire, has devised this plenary for practical and artistic subjects. She had observed how some students struggle to appreciate how far they have progressed in a lesson, so she takes a photograph of their work at the start and then puts it up on a screen at the end, so they can compare the before and after. Not only are students encouraged by how far they have come, but you can also ask them to discuss specific aspects of their work or next steps.

25. Relays for Revision

This makes for a fun and fast-paced end to a lesson. It is an effective activity for testing just how much the pupils can remember, it reviews the key learning and it encourages good team working. Divide the class into small relay teams of around four or five pupils. Give all the teams the same initial question about the topic they are studying. They must decide on an answer as a group and one of them must scribe their answer on a slip of paper.

Next, the 'runner' takes their answer up to the front desk and checks it with the teacher. If it is correct, they pick up the next question and return to their group to complete the second leg of the relay. However, if they have got the answer wrong, the teacher will provide some pointers on what they need to do to improve or highlight where they have made a mistake, and they should try the question again. Alternatively, the teacher can provide a 'help slip' with suggestions for tackling the question (which ensures that the teacher is not overwhelmed by runners requiring support). The team that has successfully completed all four questions in the shortest amount of time is the winning team. Time should be allowed at the end of the lesson to discuss any questions the pupils found problematic.

Bibliography

Agarwal, Pooja K., Patrice M. Bain and Roger W. Chamberlain (2012) The Value of Applied Research: Retrieval Practice Improves Classroom Learning and Recommendations from a Teacher, a Principal, and a Scientist. *Educational Psychology Review*, 24(3): 437–448.

Anderson, Lorin W. and David R. Krathwohl (2001) *A Taxonomy for Learning, Teaching and Assessing: A Revision of Bloom's Taxonomy of Educational Objectives* (New York: Longman).

Bentley-Davies, Caroline (2011) *Outstanding Lessons Pocketbook* (Alresford: Teachers' Pocketbooks).

Bentley-Davies, Caroline (2015) *Raising Achievement Pocketbook* (Alresford: Teachers' Pocketbooks).

Berger, Ron (2003) *An Ethic of Excellence: Building a Culture of Craftsmanship with Students* (Portsmouth, NH: Heinemann).

Bjork, Elizabeth L. and Robert Bjork (2009) Making Things Hard on Yourself, But in a Good Way: Creating Desirable Difficulty to Enhance Learning. In Morton Gernsbacher, Richard Pew, Leaette Hough and James Pomerantz (eds), *Psychology and the Real World: Essays Illustrating Fundamental Contributions to Society* (New York: Worth), pp. 56–64.

Blair, William M. (1957) President Draws Planning Moral: Recalls Army Days to Show Value of Preparedness in Time of Crisis, *New York Times* (15 November).

Broadfoot, Patricia, Richard Daugherty, John Gardner, Wynne Harlen, Mary James and Gordon Stobart (2002) *Assessment for Learning: 10 Principles. Research-Based Principles to Guide Classroom Practice Assessment for Learning* (Assessment Reform Group). Available at: https://www.researchgate.net/publication/271849158_Assessment_for_Learning_10_Principles_Research-based_principles_to_guide_classroom_practice_Assessment_for_Learning.

Busch, Bradley (2016) Great Expectations: How to Help Your Students Fulfil Their Potential, *The Guardian* (31 August). Available at: https://www.theguardian.com/teacher-network/2016/aug/31/great-expectations-how-to-help-your-students-fulfil-their-potential.

Carey, Michael P. and Andrew D. Forsyth (2009) Teaching Tip Sheet: Self-Efficacy, *American Psychological Association*. Available at: https://www.apa.org/pi/aids/resources/education/self-efficacy.

Centre for Education Statistics and Evaluation (2017) *Cognitive Load Theory: Research That Teachers Really Need to Understand* (September). Available at: https://www.cese.nsw.gov.au/publications-filter/cognitive-load-theory-research-that-teachers-really-need-to-understand.

Clarke, Shirley (2011) *Formative Assessment in the Secondary Classroom* (London: Hodder Education).

Cotton, Kathleen (1988) Classroom Questioning. School Improvement Research Series, Close-Up #5. Available at: https://educationnorthwest.org/resources/classroom-questioning.

Craig, Scotty D., Jeremiah Sullins, Amy Witherspoon and Barry Gholson (2006) The Deep-Level-Reasoning-Question Effect: The Role of Dialogue and Deep-Level-Reasoning Questions During Vicarious Learning, *Cognition and Instruction*, 24(4): 565–591.

Double, Kit, Joshua McGrane and Therese N. Hopfenbeck (2020) The Impact of Peer Assessment on Academic Performance: A Meta-Analysis of Control Group Studies, *Educational Psychology Review*, 32(1): 481–509. Available at: https://www.researchgate.net/publication/337872565_The_Impact_of_Peer_Assessment_on_Academic_Performance_A_Meta-analysis_of_Control_Group_Studies.

Dweck, Carol S. (2007) *Mindset: The New Psychology of Success* (New York: Ballantine).

Ebbinghaus, Hermann (2014 [1913]) *Memory: A Contribution to Experimental Psychology*, tr. Henry A. Ruger and Clara Bussenius (New York: Windham Press).

Eva, Amy L. (2017) Why We Should Embrace Mistakes in School, *Greater Good Magazine* (28 November). Available at: https://greatergood.berkeley.edu/article/item/why_we_should_embrace_mistakes_in_school.

Facer, Jo (2020) Why Peer Assessment Doesn't Work, *TES* (3 January). Available at: https://www.tes.com/magazine/article/why-peer-assessment-doesnt-work.

Forster, Edward M. (1951) Sayings of the Week, *The Observer* (7 October).

Glass, Arnold L. and Neha Sinha (2013) Multiple Choice Questioning is an Efficient Instructional Methodology That May Be Widely Implemented in Academic Courses to Improve Exam Performance, *Current Directions in Psychological Science*, 22(6): 471–477.

Greenfield, Susan (2016) *A Day in the Life of the Brain: The Neuroscience of Consciousness from Dawn Till Dusk* (London: Penguin).

Gross, Ronald (1999) *Peak Learning: How to Create Your Own Lifelong Education Program for Personal Enlightenment and Professional Success* (New York: Jeremy P. Tarcher/Putnam).

Hattie, John (2009) *Visible Learning: A Synthesis of Over 800 Meta-Analyses Relating to Achievement* (Abingdon and New York: Routledge).

McDaniel, Mark A., Pooja K. Agarwal, Barbie J. Huelser, Kathleen B. McDermott and Henry L. Roediger III (2011) Test-Enhanced Learning in a Middle School Science Classroom: The Effects of Quiz Frequency and Placement, *Journal of Educational Psychology*, 103(2) 399–414.

McDaniel, Mark A., Ruthann C. Thomas, Pooja K. Agarwal, Kathleen B. McDermott and Henry L. Roediger III (2012) Quizzing Promotes Transfer of Target Principles in Middle School Science: Benefits on Classroom Exams. Manuscript submitted for publication.

Marland, Michael (1975) *The Craft of the Classroom: A Survival Guide* (Oxford: Heinemann).

Mitchell, John (2016) *100 Ideas for Secondary Teachers: Revision* (London: Bloomsbury).

Nuthall, Graham (2007) *The Hidden Lives of Learners* (Wellington: New Zealand Council for Educational Research Press).

Owen, Paul (2019) Memory, *Stockport Grammar School Headmaster's Blog* (25 March). Available at: https://www.stockportgrammar.co.uk/news-and-events/news/memory.

Petty, Geoff (2009) *Evidence-Based Teaching: A Practical Approach*, 2nd rev. edn (Oxford: Oxford University Press).

Pope, Gorden (2013) *Questioning Technique Pocketbook* (Alresford: Teachers' Pocketbooks).

Ratcliffe, Susan (ed.) (2011) *Concise Oxford Dictionary of Quotations* (Oxford: Oxford University Press).

Roediger III, Henry L., Pooja K. Agarwal, Mark A. McDaniel and Kathleen B. McDermott (2011) Test-Enhanced Learning in the Classroom: Long-Term Improvements from Quizzing, *Journal of Experimental Psychology: Applied*, 17(4): 382–395.

Rosenthal, Robert and Lenore Jacobson (1968) Pygmalion in the Classroom, *Urban Review*, 3: 16–20.

Rowe, Mary Budd (1978) *Teaching Science as Continuous Inquiry: A Basic* (New York: McGraw Hill).

Rowling, Joanne K. (2008) The Fringe Benefits of Failure and the Importance of Imagination. Harvard University commencement address, 5 June. Available at: https://news.harvard.edu/gazette/story/2008/06/text-of-j-k-rowling-speech.

Smith, Jim (2017) *The Lazy Teacher's Handbook – New Edition: How Your Students Learn More When You Teach Less* (Carmarthen: Independent Thinking Press).

Wiliam, Dylan (2011) *Embedded Formative Assessment* (Bloomington, IN: Solution Tree Press).

Wiliam, Dylan (2014) Is the Feedback You're Giving Students Helping or Hindering? *Dylan Wiliam Center* (29 November). Available at: https://www.dylanwiliamcenter.com/2014/11/29/is-the-feedback-you-are-giving-students-helping-or-hindering.

Wiliam, Dylan and Paul Black (2006) *Inside the Black Box: Raising Standards through Classroom Assessment* (London: GL Assessment).

Wragg, Edward C. and George Brown (2001) *Questioning in the Secondary School* (London and New York: RoutledgeFalmer).

Wylie, Caroline and Dylan Wiliam (2006) Diagnostic Questions: Is There Value in Just One? Paper presented at the annual meeting of the American Educational Research Association and the National Council on Measurement in Education, San Francisco, CA, 6–12 April. Available at: http://www.dylanwiliam.org/Dylan_Wiliams_website/Papers_files/DIMS%20(NCME%202006).pdf.

About the Author

Caroline Bentley-Davies is an Oxford graduate who started her teaching career in Berkshire, England. She has been a middle leader in three schools, an education adviser for a local authority and is now an educational trainer across the UK and overseas.

Caroline runs revision sessions for students across the UK focused on honing their examination preparation and revision practice. She also runs training sessions for teachers on retrieval practice, metacognition and making teaching and learning 'sticky'. Her reputation means that she has been invited to speak in schools across the world, and teachers from as far afield as the United States and Russia have travelled to attend her sessions.

For more information about Caroline, please see her website: www.bentley-davies.co.uk or follow her on Twitter @RealCBD.